Who Moved My Bone?

A Guide for Multi-Dog Households

Theresa Mancuso

ADAMS MEDIA
AVON, MASSACHUSETTS

Published by
Adams Media, an F+W Publications Company
57 Littlefield Street, Avon, MA 02322. U.S.A.
www.adamsmedia.com

ISBN: 1-59337-012-1

Printed in Canada

J I H G F E D C B A

Library of Congress Cataloging-in-Publication Data
Mancuso, Theresa.
Who moved my bone? / Theresa Mancuso.
p.   cm.
ISBN 1-59337-012-1
1. Dogs. I. Title.

SF427.M265 2004
636.7--dc22
2003028018

This publication is designed to provide accurate and authoritative information
with regard to the subject matter covered. It is sold with the understanding that
the publisher is not engaged in rendering legal, accounting, or other professional advice. If legal advice or other expert assistance is required, the services
of a competent professional person should be sought.
—From a *Declaration of Principles* jointly adopted by a Committee of the
American Bar Association and a Committee of Publishers and Associations

Many of the designations used by manufacturers and sellers to distinguish their
products are claimed as trademarks. Where those designations appear in this
book and Adams Media was aware of a trademark claim, the designations have
been printed with initial capital letters.

This book is available at quantity discounts for bulk purchases.
For information, call 1-800-872-5627.

Dedicated
In memory
Of my parents
Who taught me to love and cherish
All creatures.

Acknowledgments

My heartfelt gratitude goes out to all my family and friends, fellow dog enthusiasts and professional colleagues—everyone who encouraged and supported me throughout the making of this book.

Most of all, I thank my sister, Dr. Carolina Mancuso, for her unfailing love and friendship. Her constancy as a loving mother, gifted teacher, and dedicated author, inspires me daily with the love of reading and writing and in the lifelong project of parenting those entrusted to our care.

I am indebted to all the dog breeders, trainers, and owners I have met along the way for sharing their valuable insights about all things canine, particularly: Dominic Donovan (Donovan K-9s, Newark, New Jersey), Tyril Frith (The K-9 Academy, Brooklyn, New York), Dr. Barbara "Bobbi" Geilla (The Educated Puppy, Brooklyn, New York), Elli Matlin (Highland Hills German Shepherds, Brooklyn, New York), Joe Moldovan (Training Director, Algemeiner Schutzhund Club of Long Island), John and Jane Olsson (Cedarosen Kennels, Cornville, Maine), and Sarah Slader Waldorf (Konigsdorf Kennels) who kindly wrote the foreword for this book. To all of you, my loving thanks! God bless you!

I'd like to give a big juicy bone to cover boy, Apollo, an American bulldog bred by Willie Melendez (Universal K-9, Brooklyn, New York), and owned by Ian Engberg (Brooklyn, New York). Thank you, Ian, for letting Apollo grace the cover of this book.

I would be remiss if I failed to acknowledge the encouragement and support of Jack Ryan, my editor-in-chief at the New York City Department of Probation. As a trusted friend and supervisor as well as a seasoned journalist and editor, Jack taught me a great deal about writing. His gracious interest in this project from its inception has fueled my creativity all along. An enthusiastic dog lover and father of four, Jack never tires of sharing my enthusiasm for pack life.

No writer can achieve the fulfillment of publishing a cherished work without the combined efforts of a dedicated literary agent and project editor to shepherd the manuscript along. Mine have been the best! Words do not suffice to express my appreciation to Sara Camilli, my literary agent, for her dauntless efforts on my behalf. Her brilliant sense of humor and limitless talents make her the answer to an author's prayer, and this one feels singularly blessed in having found her. Thanks to Kate Epstein, my project editor at Adams Media, for her painstaking assistance in shaping and honing this book.

Finally, my love and appreciation for the heart and soul of this project, my furry muses, the magnificent four-legged companions with whom I share my life. My pack has taught me everything and given me much more, besides. Thank you, New Skete's Natasha ("Tash"); Alexander Nevsky of Night Hawk ("Sasha"); Cara Mia vom Ennishaus ("Cara Mia"); Grip von der Starken ("Grip"); Geist von der Starken ("Geisty"); Maximus; Nikki; Primo; and, last but not least, Marmaduke Rodgers.

Contents

Foreword

I have known Theresa Mancuso for some fifteen years. In that time, I have found her to possess great insight, not only as to what makes our canine companions tick, but what we can do to help them be happy members of our family "packs." Included in this carefully crafted work are the answers to questions that new and seasoned dog owners alike continually ask when they consider adding a second or third dog to their home: "Is a male or a female better for our family?" "How do I introduce the new puppy into the home?" "Why shouldn't I get two puppies at one time?" If you are fortunate enough to have purchased your puppy (or dog) from a knowledgeable breeder, nearly every question you would ask them is addressed in this book.

Dogs are dogs, and people are people. Understanding the way dogs view the world, what dogs expect from your leadership, and how dogs naturally interact will greatly assist you in forming a happy and harmonious "family pack." There is more to life with dogs than attending a training class, and the more you understand about your hounds, the greater your mutual enjoyment. We can learn a lot from our animal family.

It is said that a person is fortunate who has one truly good friend in a lifetime. As dog people, we consider ourselves fortunate to have shared our lives with *one* very special dog. How much greater, then, is the incredible good fortune of those who have experienced the friendship of several outstanding canines? Pack life, as Theresa suggests, is something above and beyond the ordinary dog experience. As such, it merits a particular consideration. When we live with a pack, we have many best friends.

Sometimes we raise these special souls from their puppy days, but sometimes they come to us as rescues or as older dogs that somehow find their way into our hearts. Pack dogs reach us from many sources, but each one has its own story, and each one is a special member of the family. Our dogs are always living life "in the moment," and when we take the time to join them there, the rewards are great. Whatever the ages or shapes of your dogs, you can be sure that great dogs make great teachers.

Welcome to the world of dogs and dog people. You have come to the right place. May your enjoyment be as great as your teachers'.

—Sarah Slader Waldorf, M.S., Ed.,
Konigsdorf German Shepherds

Introduction

In a perfect world, every dog would have a home
and every home would have a dog—or maybe several.
—Unknown

S ince we humans first welcomed canines into our midst,
dogs have served us well, providing pleasure and protection to people of every time and place, from those
who dwelled in caves to those who live in the world's busiest
cities. Modern man depends on dogs for companionship and
for personal assistance of all descriptions, including seeing eye
dogs, service dogs for paraplegics, and therapy dogs for the
elderly and disabled. Dogs also do serious work for the police
and military, performing important tasks such as bomb sniffing,
search and rescue, criminal tracking, and guard work. Of all
the sentient beings on earth, only dogs—with their undaunted
love and loyalty—are known as man's best friend.

The love we share with our canine companions so greatly
enriches our lives that often, one dog is just not enough! We
find ourselves in need of doubling our pleasure or tripling it.
Soon, we are parenting a canine pack.

This book is about raising dogs together in a pack and
living with them like a family. It's about maintaining (and surviving!) a multi-dog home. Such a lifestyle, of course, is not for
everyone. Not everyone wishes to be or even can be a multi-
dog owner. It takes a relatively unusual person to make such
a commitment. But for those of us who belong to this group,
it's hard to imagine being happy any other way.

This book is for multi-dog owners, the parents of the pack. It is written for those hardy individuals who love the challenge of living with more than one dog. It's a how-to guide for folks who grin and say, "One is not enough!" Our goal is to provide guidance to anyone who's thinking of becoming a multi-dog owner. For pack parents, daily life is filled with awesome challenges and rich rewards. How to reap the rewards by surviving the challenges is the ever-unfolding learning experience that comes with living with dogs.

Keeping a multi-dog home is a special kind of life, which is not for the faint-hearted or selfish. Dogs are *not* children; "they are," as Henry Beston wrote in *The Outermost House,* "other nations, caught with us in the great web of time." Nevertheless, there's a childlike quality in many dogs. That's why I refer to multi-dog owners as "pack parents." Dogs are *like* children except that children grow up to become responsible adults, while dogs can never be completely independent or self-supporting. Nevertheless, well-trained canines have proven themselves remarkably responsible. Numerous true-life reports describe events in which dogs took responsibility to save their masters or others from danger and death. Children in families with dogs have an added margin of safety and security, as well as priceless interspecies companionship.

Dogs require lots of care, but in exchange, they give us blessings money can't buy. Our children mature and create more children, and if we're lucky, they might take care of us in our old age. Although dogs will certainly make more dogs if we let nature take its course, they'll never help you pay the rent or push your wheelchair. What they will do, what they *always* do, is give you unconditional love, constancy and loyalty, forgiveness, and absolute acceptance. They are the best friends you'll ever have. Dogs are completely incorruptible, totally without malice, and unbelievably valiant—in short, a constant example of what we, too, should be.

Dogs must learn how to live with their human families, as part of a real neighborhood and subject to the conditions of this world of ours. It's our duty to train them to behave properly wherever they are. Caring for our canines doesn't ever end, regardless of their maturity. Throughout their lives, from infancy to old age, they need our support and care. They depend on us as their human parents for everything in their lives. It's up to us to secure their safety, health, and happiness and to enable them to fulfill their purpose in the world. Dogs give back to us a thousandfold by enriching our lives every single day. They ensure *our* safety, enable our health, and deepen our happiness. It is a bargain, the like of which is unequaled in the marketplace of human experience. If you regard dogs as merchandise or commodities, this is not the book for you. Dogs are incredibly magnificent creatures, perhaps just a little less than angels. They have real feelings and thoughts—albeit unspoken in human language—profoundly worthy of our respect. A decent human being would never hurt a dog deliberately. If you're with me so far, I hope this book will help you as much as living with the pack has helped me.

When you love a single dog, it's easy to love two or three or more. Puppies in particular have the power to weasel their way into our hearts before we realize what it means to have a second, third, or fourth canine in the circle of our home. This book is about figuring out the inner workings of your furry children, what makes dogs tick, and how best to manage the pack. To live well in the midst of dogs, you must be their leader or alpha. You must integrate your dog life into the rest of your life, work, family, hobby and sport, so that harmony and balance emerge. As you journey through this book, you'll find yourself a little wiser, a little stronger, and much more capable and determined to enjoy the challenges of your multi-dog home.

Although I'm not a medical professional, I took the liberty of including elements of all facets of my research, experience, and consultation. As a consequence, this book includes brief discussions about health and nutrition, holistic and homeo-pathic dog care and herbs for pets, and first aid for dogs. This is not a training manual, but you will find here some useful training techniques. To live successfully with dogs, we must train them, for if we don't, then it's a sure thing that they'll train one another and us, too! As the late humorist Corey Ford said, "Properly trained, a man can be dog's best friend."

My passion for dogs has prompted me through four decades to gather unto myself many canine friends, both in my own family pack and elsewhere, through training, play, and work. It's been a glorious, fulfilling experience. With great respect for this marvelous species, let me share with you some of the information I have gleaned while loving dogs and living closely with them. I hope this book helps you enjoy your dogs more fully and take care of them more effectively. May you and your pack live long and prosper.

—Theresa Mancuso

chapter 1

Is Pack Life
Right for You?

One dog barks at something; the rest bark at him.
—Chinese Proverb

Dog ownership is a serious responsibility as well as a lot of fun. Pack ownership may double or triple the responsibility, but it exponentially increases the pleasure. Multi-dog types may find themselves drifting closer toward becoming pack parents as soon as their first furry friend has mastered the basics. One dog is wonderful, you might reflect; how much more so would several be! You notice people walking several dogs at a time. The rhythm on those leashes tugs at your mind and heart. Those beautiful canines trotting proudly beside their person move in an aura of magic, with a kind of pizzazz that draws your attention and locks on your heart. The idea takes root, and you find yourself leaning hard toward getting another dog.

You talk it over with friends and family members, this inclination you have to get another dog. For the most part, you expect them to nix the idea. It's only the *other* multi-doggers who openly and shamelessly cheer you on. "Yeah, yeah, go for it," they say. A few conscientious souls warn you that managing more than one dog at a time can pose some problems, but the gung-ho others insist there's nothing like it, nothing better than having a few dogs around the house. The more you think of it, the more you want it. It's luring you like a spell straight to the kennel or pound. You've got to have another canine.

Believe me, friend, I know the feeling. You're not alone. There are plenty of us out here who can never get enough dog.

If you're thinking about becoming a multi-dogger, don't rush into it. Stop and ask yourself a few questions:

- Do I have enough time to devote to a second or third dog?
- Can I afford the financial responsibility of veterinary care for an additional dog or more? Can I afford to feed more canines?
- Is there sufficient space in my home to provide adequately for pack life?
- Who will do the walking? Cleaning up after? Training? Supervising?
- Is my first and present dog sufficiently prepared to have a sibling? How well trained is dog number one?
- Am I ready for the pack lifestyle?

A Commitment of Time

If you want a second or third canine, take a realistic look at your twenty-four-hour days. Puppies need more time than older dogs. Neither pups nor adult dogs know about clocks and calendars. Nevertheless, all dogs seem to have an innate understanding of the days and times important to them. They know when to get up, when to eat and drink, when to do "business," and when to play. If you work away from home, they know exactly when you should return at the end of the day. Dogs possess an uncanny ability to know if this particular day is a holiday, a day off, or a day when you are *theirs* for a much longer period.

If you have a dog and you want to get a second or third, time is a major consideration. Your regular schedule, neatly affording ample time for your first canine buddy, will have to expand a little to include sufficient hours to provide for the pack. Everything you do for and with your single dog will be doubled or tripled. Ask those who know, the multi-doggers who have committed their time and resources to pack life. They will regale you with the delights of double dogging, but they will also affirm that it takes a lot of time to do it right. If you want pack life, be prepared to dedicate as much time as it takes to do it fairly, consistently, and throughout the full life cycle of each and every dog in your household.

Regardless of whether you have a backyard, you must be willing to go out and take long, invigorating walks every day, not once, but twice every single day, rain or shine, snow, sleet, or wind. When it's hot and when it's cold, dogs need their walks. Not only do dogs need regular walks to relieve themselves, but a good walk also provides the mental, emotional, and physical stimulation that keeps them healthy and happy. When dogs are banished to the backyard, they usually just lie about and doze. They do not exercise or interact much, unless, of course, you're out there, too, energizing them with a game. Owning more than one dog doesn't mean you have to increase the amount of time you spend with each, but you have to include the second, third, and fourth dog in a meaningful way so that everyone in the pack gets plenty of exercise and attention. Creative planning and use of time will help you reap the wonderful rewards of pack life.

Having three large dogs for twelve years, I never felt overburdened in my daily routine, and every dog fully participated in the life of the pack every day. For those of you who are parents of human children, think about how much time you had to add to your family life with the arrival of your new baby. From this perspective, it's kind of a crazy question—you simply live, don't you? Every child takes its place and life goes on. You don't think about increasing your family time by 50 percent or more for each new sibling that enlarges the human pack. Nor do you need to double or triple your time investment with more dogs; you just have to keep yourself willing and open to changes in the way you schedule your life.

Financial Responsibility

I'm proud to be among the doggie poor. There's no use denying it. I've spent the greater part of three decades taking care of one, two, or three dogs, large German shepherds with bottomless pits for stomachs. I've invested in an endless supply of pet toys, individual dog crates, a Schutzhund sleeve for bite work, leashes, collars, and harnesses. I've made sure the best veterinarians I could find treated my dogs.

Dogs need regular trips to the veterinarian, and each dog on occasion may require additional visits. Vets are not cheap. Neither is high-quality dog food. Feeding and vetting dogs is a major financial responsibility.

You're probably a responsible working adult. You might also be a kid who desperately wants a second or third dog. Or perhaps you're a retired senior with a weakness for strays, picking them up and taking them home with you. Regardless of your age or station, being a multi-dog owner is a big-time financial responsibility. Don't let me scare you. It's not about being rich, but if you want a dog-pack family, be prepared to make some real sacrifices. There will definitely be times when the care of your dogs will require you to pass up spending money on something for yourself. A good parent knows how to make sacrifices, and a good pack parent has to learn the same lesson. So let's be realistic about it. Even if you adopt the second dog and do not pay a huge breeder's fee, there will still be basic financial outlays for vet care and feeding. Yes, dog lover/addict, the truth is that it costs more to keep two or three dogs than it does to keep one. On the other hand, you also benefit by the use of hand-me-down toys, leashes, collars, and other such items. Additionally, there's the financial incentive of purchasing dog food wholesale.

I've never let money stand in the way of my passion for dogs, but that's because I'm an inveterate, incorrigible doggie addict. I have to have a dog. In fact, I have to have several! If that's *your* passion too, just spend less money on yourself. Forget about fancy vacations, beautiful clothes, dinners out, and other niceties—unless of course, you can afford it all! For those of us who are pack addicts, the joy of dogs is well worth the sacrifices we make to maintain them. When love is the driving force, there's no such thing as sacrifice.

Space for a Pack

Seeing me walk my pack, people without dogs often ask, "Where do you keep them? Do you have a big house? A yard?" Having dogs is easier in a sizeable dwelling. Having a back-yard is wonderful. But the pack can thrive just as well in an apartment, as mine has always done, as in a mansion. Each dog only occupies as large a volume of space as its body requires. Dogs nest happily on an old couch or chair, or, if you permit them—though trainers discourage it—on your bed. (Pick your trainers carefully, lest they influence your personal preferences and those of the dogs. My dogs would never forgive me if I listened to trainers or training manuals that say, "Off!")

Dogs are easy to please. When at home, most dogs fold their supple bodies into prone postures, jowls flat to the floor, while their adoring eyes follow you wherever you go. Of course, larger dogs need more space. You can't box them into a space so limited that they will overturn tables, chairs, and lamps just trying to move. Regardless of their size, your dogs need a suitable place for feeding. You also need adequate storage space in a multi-dog home. An extra room, closet, or hallway works well for keeping large bags of dog food, feeding utensils, collars, leashes, toys, and training gear out of the way.

You also need floor space sufficient to accommodate as many dog crates as you have dogs in the pack. Each dog gets its own crate, each one big enough that the dog can stand, sit, or turn about while inside. All dogs need a safe "little cave" for time out, and crates make great meditation chambers. Keep your dog crates in a central part of your home, whether in the kitchen, living room, or your workspace. Secluded areas like the back hall are like banishment to Siberia for loving family pets. They need to see what's going on. After all, crating is not punishment. It's just a way to get dogs to calm down and desist from their daffy dogness.

Most important, keep in mind that dogs are happiest with the person they love. Whether in a tiny apartment or a huge mansion, dogs of any size can enjoy a marvelous life together. All they need is their human alpha, sufficient good food, and vigorous daily exercise.

Who Will Do the Work?

Presumably, you already know the drill that comes with single dog ownership. You have to feed the critter, walk him, groom him, train him, supervise him, and bed him down at night with a firm command to seek his place and stay there: "Go to bed, Jasper, now!" Every additional dog requires about the same amount of time as your first dog does, but you can do all the necessary doggie things with the whole pack just as you would in a family of children. There's no need to repeat the same procedures endlessly with each dog. Pack life, like family life, has its own natural rhythm. Some pack owners prefer walking each dog separately, but I don't, and I don't recommend it either. We lead busy lives, and our dogs can adjust quite easily. Make your own decision about what works best for you, but understand that dogs learn from each other. Pack life is a great teacher. It's not necessary to go through each step exactly as you did with your first dog. But, if you did it all wrong the first time around, here's your chance to change history!

So who will do the work? Are you a single person living alone? Are you part of a couple? With or without children? Do you work full time? Is your job done at home or away from home? How do you spend evenings and weekends? What time do you get up and go to bed? These are real questions and concern real issues for the multi-dog parent.

Our dogs are completely at our mercy, totally dependent upon us for food, shelter, exercise, security, and safety. In short, the pack needs us for its survival. Dogs thrive on routine, and routine makes animal care much easier. Before the pack is actually assembled, make a plan for regular walks, grooming, training, clean up, and overall supervision. Most of this really means doing what comes naturally. Only when we humans fail to meet nature's reasonable demands with wisdom and responsibility does life fall apart at the seams.

Is Your Present Dog Ready for a Sibling?

Herein lies the rub. Your success as a pack parent will mirror the way you handle your current dog. If you've properly trained your present pooch, more likely than not, you'll be a

successful (and sane) multi-dog owner. One of the most important questions to ask yourself before acquiring another dog
concerns the dog you already have. Is your present dog ready
for a sibling? How can you tell?

Take the time to regularly review basic obedience with
your dog. Strive for reliability in the come, sit, down, and stay
exercises since newcomers quickly will follow the example of
the Original Pup. Group obedience drills are great for new
members of the pack, but only if the first ones obey properly.

Original Pup must be well-socialized before you introduce
another dog into the household. Socialization is the ongoing
process of teaching dogs how to behave during encounters
with others, both human and canine. The work of socializing
a dog extends throughout its lifetime, becoming easier as the
dog matures and has many experiences under its belt. If your
dog is reasonably well-behaved around other dogs and is tolerant of new situations, have no fear of acquiring another furry
critter. But if your dog pulls, barks, scratches, and digs like a
mischievous monster, you should seriously work to cure these
problems before you bring a newcomer into the scene. New
pack members tend to copy what they see around them, and
that means the bad stuff as well as the good.

Puppies and young dogs need plenty of opportunities to
meet strangers. They must learn to become accustomed to
strange sights and sounds. They need to walk on different
types of pavement, grass, dirt, rock, sand, and the iron gratings
on sidewalks. Experience with these things, plus your constant
encouragement, helps the dog achieve self-confidence.
Temperament tests require dogs to walk on variable types of
underfoot materials and to encounter surprises, such as an
umbrella springing open unexpectedly in front of the dog. By
making your dog accustomed from an early age to going

confidently wherever you go, the dog will be calm in meeting unusual experiences. It will not balk or run away. If, so far, your dog only walks on pavement or grass, try to accustom it to new and different footings.

The purpose of this in relation to pack management is to create a solid foundation in each dog before adding a new dog to the mix. The pack's encounters with the world will be strengthened proportionately. But if you haven't done the basics yet, your canine buddy is most likely not quite ready to have a buddy of its own. Correct these deficits before progressing to pack life.

Are You Ready to Be a Pack Parent?

If you're still reading, you're down to the most significant concern of all: yourself. Are you ready? Should you do it? Can you do it? How will you live in your multi-dog home? How shall you parent the pack?

You can be a successful pack parent in all sorts of settings. You don't need a Ph.D., but you do need an abundance of patience and determination, a strong sense of purpose, a deep abiding love for dogs, and the willingness to learn from your mistakes (of which there will probably be many!). When I got my first second dog—and even more so with the third—I was very nervous about what I had committed myself to do, and I had many second thoughts about it. Facing the challenge of my first multi-dog home gave me many moments of consternation. But it's the nature of dogs to thrive in the pack, for they are essentially pack animals. And thrive they did! For *you* to thrive in the pack, you must be capable of strong leadership and consistent control. You might not have all of this down pat to begin with, but you'll learn a lot as you go along. The dogs themselves will teach you.

Becoming a pack parent requires a passionate willingness to face what lies before you. You are responsible for forging the pack; making your home pack-proof so it will be safe and secure for your canine brood; and committing yourself to the daily grind of hard work, training, grooming, feeding, cleaning, and loving several boisterous dogs at the same time. The pleasures of the dog life that beckon you will make it all worthwhile. Nevertheless, if you can't commit wholeheartedly for the long haul, as long as each one of your dogs shall live, it's better not to do it at all. But if you've got the grit to go for it, oh, the joy of awakening to the sound of barking dogs or feeling their silent wet noses nudging against your cheek; of hearing the swish of wagging tails and watching those happy bodies run through open fields as a single motion of being, to live in the depth of nature no matter where you are—that's the joy of dogs.

Are you ready for the thrill of pack ownership? Do you feel your own call of the wild, the persistent gut-level anticipation of the next new pup and the next after that one? If the answer is yes, then now's the time. Go for it.

Pack Mentality and the Alpha Dog

Pack mentality is natural to dogs. Your dog considers you and other family members as its pack. When you add a second and third dog to the mix, the characteristics of the canine pack emerge, many of which we'll speak about in the pages ahead. Living in a multi-dog home is like having a pack within a pack, the canine group in the human family.

Pack mentality is genetic. Wolves often live as couples in the wilderness pack. Female wolves have been observed helping to care for youngsters without regard to whether the offspring are their own. Life is perpetuated on the principle of mutual survival. This is ensured by the strength of the pack, which is dependent upon the hierarchy in which alpha male or female reigns supreme. In a multi-dog home, the owner *must* be the alpha. Everything depends upon it.

The pack structure grows and develops as more dogs are added. One will emerge as alpha, the top dog. The others, recognizing this, show respectful obeisance without becoming subservient. If you observe a litter of puppies during their first few months of life, you will readily spot the alpha male and alpha female. Top dogs stand out by virtue of their superior strength and confidence. Even in pursuit of their mother's nursing teats, the infant alpha makes sure to get its meal by the most vigorous pursuit of the fountain of food. Alpha pup is also usually the first guy out of the whelping box.

The alpha characteristic of powerful resilience works well in the wild, and it can help you with your domestic pack if you know how to harness its superiority. The well-trained alpha is second to none, always ready to investigate and quick to act. Because the others accept alpha's position as top dog, the pack has cohesion and security and readily submits to alpha's influence, for better or for worse. You can't afford to let an alpha male or female compete with you for your alpha position. Top dog in the pack will respect the human alpha as long as you are firm and consistent, fair and steadfast in exercising your authority. If you continue to reinforce their training, your pack will maintain its hierarchy and will not threaten human authority, but it's all up to you in the final analysis. You are the one who sets the pace for everything.

The alpha doesn't need to achieve pack supremacy by fighting, maiming, or killing. Nor should the alpha human resort to any kind of extreme or severe punishment.

At the same time, there might be some physical struggle among your dogs at first, especially when you add newcomers. But afterwards, they accept their hierarchical places and peace prevails. Dogs work these things out best without human interference, but vigilance is still necessary.

Sometimes a young male will try to assert itself as it approaches puberty. The teenager might challenge the older dogs, including the alpha. If the older dog, even an alpha, is no longer physically capable of putting up a good fight, the younger will prevail and become the new top dog. That's the way nature provides for the handing down of top-dog status. Dogs usually work these things out by themselves, but sometimes you might have to intervene. Be firm, fair, and resourceful in administering discipline to dogs, and don't be afraid to do so. Separate the fighters if serious injury seems likely. Dogs, like children, require a steady hand, not a heavy one. They know you're the boss, so keep it that way.

If things get too rough, you might have to grab the worst aggressor by the tail from behind and pull it away from the fight, while at the same time giving a strong-voiced verbal correction. Don't put your face in front of their faces, and don't try to reason with them. Exercise as much physical force as needed, but do so prudently. Be aware that you could be bitten, so be careful. Throwing cold water (if you have some) on agitated dogs sometimes helps bring them back to their senses. I have never feared breaking up fighting dogs. My pack always knows I'm the boss.

It helps if there is someone else to control the other dog, but you could find yourself in a situation where you have to take action alone. It's up to you to judge each event as it happens. This is an area in which your alpha skills must come to the fore. Sometimes, it works to just call one or all of them by name and walk away. Many dogs will leave off fighting to follow their alpha human. (I'm not talking about super-tough, hard-nosed working dogs here but ordinary run-of-the-mill family pets.)

Leader of the Pack

The pack bond is very tight. If you're not absolutely alpha yourself, the canine alpha will quickly surpass you in authority over the group. Then your words will have little impact on pack behavior. The dogs are likely to just ignore you and go their merry way, for better or for worse. I have seen the results of people losing control of their dogs by failing to establish and maintain their authority in the pack. Not a pleasant experience, but it did reinforce my conviction that human alpha status is very important in a multi-dog home. The pack owners I've observed who lost control either sought help and corrected their own mistakes or eventually gave up the idea of maintaining several dogs. Such people might try to dissuade you from having your own multi-dog family, but don't let them scare you. You can be boss if you stick with the program and persevere as human alpha so the pack will respect and obey you.

From day one, be sure you instill a strong sense of your leadership. That's something dogs relate to naturally and willingly. Be consistent and fair with each dog from the beginning, and always require reasonable obedience from the pack by training and maintaining fair discipline. This will keep your alpha status strong and secure. The furry alpha male or female will be like a second lieutenant if it respects you. Otherwise, it will keep trying to take over as top dog. You'll find yourself unable to enforce commands without resorting to physical punishment, the worst thing you can do to dogs.

Pack Consciousness: Theirs and Yours

It's amazing how dogs seem to know where all their family members are, canine and human. But, if you must teach them to maintain pack consciousness, try this routine. At feeding time, call the dogs and walk away, carrying the food. Let them sniff it first to arouse interest. They must follow you to get to their food bowls. Wait for them to come and sit in front of you or lead them to their crates and wait for them to go inside. Give them praise and then their bowls. Hungry dogs cooperate the best in this little training activity. Every time you feed the pack, make them follow you somewhere before they can get the food.

Outdoors, when dogs are running free (in a safe place with no traffic or bicycles), do the same thing. For food, water, or a toy they love, call the pack and walk away. Don't ever go to the dogs—because that creates the game of "get away," and they will always delight in outrunning you. Make them come to you, and let it be a happy experience that results in a treat or a game. When dogs get so involved in other fun that they lose sight of you, clap your hands, send out a high-pitched call, jump, or run off to get their attention. Once they reach your side, reward them. These techniques always work if the dogs really want what you have to offer. Food or treat training has positive results, and you see the benefits immediately. If your pack does not seem tempted by food, you might just be offering the wrong kind. Try something very smelly, like a piece of cheese or turkey. Once they get a good whiff, the most inveterate will usually be motivated. Dogs get bored with the same old thing, so vary the treats you offer.

You can also improve pack consciousness by doing this little exercise. When the pack's attention is elsewhere, walk away, and hide somewhere adjacent to where they are playing. Then call them. Give a rousing whistle or other signal they know, and watch them frisk about in search of you, noses wiggling upward as they air-scent for the boss. Give them a reward when they find you. Keep the disappearance routine fairly simple until the pack completely understands the routine and develops some skill in locating you. Usually, top dog's nose goes into action first, and the others follow once your scent is caught upon the wind.

Eventually, the pack will learn to be conscious of your presence no matter what else is going on. After a while, you won't be able to sneak away from them even if you try. Once engaged, dogs can maintain pack consciousness quite naturally, but people often don't. You must school yourself to stay aware of the pack at all times. You have to know where they are and what they are doing, lest any member of the pack get injured or into trouble. This serious responsibility doesn't subtract from the enjoyment of pack life; it simply enriches it.

One for All and All for One

Pack mentality forges the whole group of dogs into a single defensive team when outsiders try to crash the pack. Older members of the pack often are protective of the younger ones, and when large dogs fight, the scuffle can become dangerous. I have seen this happen with otherwise peaceful animals. If you take your pack to any area where dogs run free off leash, be careful and attentive to their behavior. It's one of the primary responsibilities of pack ownership to be alert and ready to intervene decisively when untoward things occur. If you're a fearful person and you hesitate because you think your own dogs might bite you in the fray, you'll hardly be able to maintain sufficient authority to get your dogs out of and away from trouble. Timid folks should stick to smaller, more manageable dogs.

If you have a multi-dog household, you're responsible for keeping the dogs safe at home and elsewhere. My three large German shepherds were powerful animals and looked quite formidable running together. Despite their sound characters and calm temperaments, and the fact that they were well-trained, they could scare the wits out of smaller dogs and their owners. In deference to others, I stopped going to the public park. Instead, I took my pack to run in an open field at the city limits several times a week. All users have equal rights in public places, so pack owners must respect other dogs and their owners. There are certain times and places where you just can't turn the pack loose and hope for the best.

Gift of the Pack

Pack life is not for the faint of heart, but it sure does offer enormous rewards. There's nothing as beautiful as the choreography of several dogs on the run, a powerful well-muscled pack flying through an open field or plunging into the surf. I have relished the sight of them, traveling single-file like wolves in the wilderness, alpha dog in the lead. Running swiftly through the falling snow or tracking intensely despite a blazing sun, the sight of my pack has thrilled me with a taste of time-lessness in the wild. I watch them with mystical fascination as they go their way, sniffing surrounding bushes, marking the territory, bounding easily up a rocky terrain and coming to stand on the summit of a bluff beside me, noses lifted to sniff the offshore wind. Sometimes they howl, yodel, bark, or yelp, and the air is suddenly filled with the noise of their excitement. Pack life has been so right for me, a priceless gift that opened portals to people and places I never would have met otherwise.

Living with the pack is a powerful bond that joins you to nature as nothing else can. This vigorous interaction with dogs was profoundly healing to me during the most difficult period in my life. Choosing a multi-dog home might not be right for everybody, but if it's right for you, the gift of the pack will be yours for the taking. Dogs in a multi-dog family are double trouble or double fun, a triple challenge or a triple joy. It all depends on how you raise them and how consistently you keep the rules and show them that you mean it. They must keep them, too.

There's a mystical and deeply spiritual aspect of pack life, an experience beyond words. I probably owe my health and sanity to the dogs of my original pack, three German shepherds, Cara Mia, Grip, and Geist. They showed me their true selves and helped me rediscover mine. With them, I found my place in the world, enjoying simple things and pursuing creative work. Dogs will help you find yourself if you let them. After many years of being a nun, I had left my religious community. I felt myself adrift in the universe, alone and uncertain, not knowing which way to go. So, I went to the dogs! With them and through them, I embarked on the creation of a new and meaningful existence. It was the gift of my pack that helped me get on with life.

Living with the pack required some help, at least in the beginning. I turned to books and people who knew how to train dogs. I worked with several trainers and finally joined a local Schutzhund club. This was a sporting group devoted to dog training in obedience, tracking, and protection. I attended training and breed seminars in the United States and Canada, for I had much to learn and I knew it. As I read and studied about dogs, I watched my own constantly as they began to teach me. I was an eager student. In our life together, I came to appreciate the interaction of animals in a pack: how the older ones tolerate and teach the young, how males and females mirror one another and provide the balance and harmony of their nature. The gift of the pack is a chance to learn deeply about yourself and the wonderful world of dogs.

The pack you create will forge its own cohesive structure and generate powerful energy of its own. Pack life manifests something of nature's boundless wisdom, a reality we must respect in order to live in harmony within ourselves and with the rest of the universe. The multi-dog home is a never-ending opportunity for contemplation. The give-and-take of the pack is a reflection of the expanding universe, where all life forms give and take as they merge in the changing rhythms of evolution.

The pack possesses all the necessary elements for canine survival, and they are always operative. These are the instinctual drives that rise to the surface many times a day. We can see this natural harmony in pack life. It can be ours, too, but only if we pay attention. At the monastery at New Skete, New York, the brothers are world-respected trainers and breeders of German shepherds. As Brother Thomas of New Skete once said, "We must listen to the dogs and not hasten to impose our will upon them." By listening, we shall learn. "Ask the animals and they will teach you"; so it says in the Book of Job.

The innate wisdom at the heart of all creation possesses its own harmony. That same wisdom holds the pack together, establishes order, and enables dogs to live among themselves and with humans as family. By recognizing this and appreciating it, we can find and maintain the same wise harmony within ourselves, enabling our entire being to resonate with all of nature. This is the true gift of the pack. Pack life is a natural laboratory wherein we can study the essence of dogness and get a good look at ourselves, too, in the process.

Chapter 2

Creating a Canine Family

Whoever said you can't buy
happiness forgot about puppies.
—Gene Hill

Remember when you got your first dog? If you acquired your first when you were a youngster, chances are that you had plenty of adult help in selecting, raising, and training your dog. This was your first canine pal, the beginning of a lifelong friendship, and—in most cases—the start of a lifelong love for dogs. Becoming a pack parent begins with the first dog you ever own, even if you're just a kid yourself. Kids can be great dog parents, but they often need adult support and encouragement to do so. Having a dog creates a special opportunity to develop children's nurturing capability.

Acquiring Dogs

Dogs can be acquired from many sources, the most reliable of which is a reputable breeder. Such a breeder knows the bloodlines of his or her stock and will gladly talk you through the process of deciding on a dog. It was my good fortune to meet Ellinore Matlin of Highland Hills German Shepherds more than twenty-five years ago. Elli's mother was a dog breeder and shower before her, so Elli grew up with dogs. There's nothing she doesn't know about them. Best of all, she is always willing to share her firsthand knowledge. And share she did. I learned a great deal from Elli Matlin. Seek out a reputable breeder who loves dogs and can help you understand the characteristics of the best one for your lifestyle. Whether you want a puppy or an adult, and regardless of the breed you choose, finding a reputable source will ensure that you get a good dog and help down the road if you need it. (Naturally, breeders are in business to sell dogs, but that will not prevent the honest ones from giving you straightforward answers and good advice.) Serious breeders want to satisfy their customers, so take your time and find one you trust. Check out breed magazines and general dog-related journals. Don't rush to pick your pup without carefully considering the place and people from whom you acquire it. Breeders who are committed to their breed(s) strive to preserve and develop certain desirable types that have become established in the species. Breeding with integrity protects and promotes the welfare of the breed and the individual animal. Unfortunately, not all dog breeders are equally dedicated.

Pet-store purchases should be avoided. The puppies and dogs sold in pet stores are almost always bred in puppy mills and shipped great distances under poor conditions. Furthermore, you cannot see the parents of pet-store pups. Temperament and physical health might be at stake. Word-of-mouth referrals from people who have dealt satisfactorily with breeders and shelter folk are the best way to find the dog of your dreams.

Caretakers in animal shelters are eager to get good homes for their charges. When visiting a shelter, be prepared to see the look of sadness, hope, heartache, loneliness, and despondency in the eyes of dogs. It is heartbreaking. Many beautiful pets languish in animal shelters. You should know that a secondhand dog may well be the best canine investment of your life. Shelter pets make wonderful loving companions. Give serious thought to adoption before you conclude your search. Spend time with the dog you want before you take it home with you.

Your final option is giving a home to a stray. This is a little risky, but I know many strays that were taken from the street by wonderful people and became the best dogs they ever had. If you're inexperienced, take it slowly in selecting a pet. Be aware that strays might have been abused and could have some problems, but go with your heart all the same. Don't be afraid to give a dog a chance. Kindness often pays off. The choice is yours. No matter what some "experts" say, I cannot bring myself to suggest that anyone refuse to assist a lost or abandoned animal.

Don't be afraid to ask for help when you need it. Selecting your dog is a very important process. In the long run, you'll be glad you did, and so will the source person from whom you obtain the best dog for your lifestyle.

Many excellent books and articles are published every year to help people select and raise a puppy. A little research at the start will enable you to find the best dog for you. You are the one who will live with it, so find the dog you really want. Taking a dog into your home should be a lifetime commitment, so choose wisely, not on an emotional whim. Impulse purchases often end in disaster for the animal. When dogs fail, it's usually the person's fault, not the dog's.

Find out as much as you can about the breed and individual dog that interests you. If you plan to adopt a shelter pet, try to learn what you can about its home of origin and why it was turned in to the shelter. Shelter pets long for human companionship, especially if they once had a decent home. Street-born dogs are often street smart and adapt well to a new home with appropriate guidance and care.

If you got your first dog later in life, as an adult, you've been through this process. Most likely, you know well how to pick out and raise a dog. Whether you go to a shelter or to a reputable breeder to find the dog of your dreams, your first choice is about its size and sex. Usually, a male and female, rather than two same-gender dogs, do best together from their very first encounter. By the time you get your third dog, you'll undoubtedly have mastered the art of pack handling. When you choose between male and female at this point, you should have a better understanding of compatibility in doubling up on gender in the pack. I have found females to be far easier, so I suggest that if you want a three-dog home, let two of them be female. But pack parent friends have told me that their multi-dog homes work out just fine with all males. Some have three or four large males and they say gender doesn't matter—but usually and wisely, these boys are neutered.

Male dogs are usually more aggressive than females because of their historic place in pack life as watcher, pro-tector, and leader. Females are more homebody types. They are less likely to roam and generally less aggressive, though they can be very protective of their pups. Housebreaking females seems to be easier.

If you want your pack to be a deterrent against burglars or muggers, forget about small dogs, yappers though they be. Focus on the larger breeds, particularly working stock with strong instinctual drives. Mid-weight dogs, those of about 25 to 50 pounds, might be some deterrent, but they are hardly strong enough to protect you in serious danger. Dogs weighing more than 70 pounds make powerful allies, but also require strong arms and voice to manage correctly.

Pack selection is a matter of personal taste. Every dog has merit, and every dog deserves an owner to love and care for it throughout its life. Think through your own criteria and come to your decision. One thing is for certain: Whatever dog you take into your home will find its way into your heart.

Remember that a dog's commitment to you lasts forever and yours should, too. It's going to be at least a ten-year partnership, maybe more.

Think about your answers to the following questions to help you choose the best dog for your lifestyle:

- **Which "dog look" pleases you?** Short and squatty? Tall and slender? Heavy bone or light? Do you want the big hunky type or a svelte shapely canine? You'll see that dog every day for many years, so get one that has the look you like.

- **What kind of coat do you prefer?** Short hair or long? Keeping a dog's coat in condition is every owner's duty and every dog's right. Dogs with thick coats or long coats and those with dense undercoats—German shepherds, collies, Bernese mountain dogs—require regular brushing. Such breeds shed a great deal, while close-coated dogs like Dobermans and hounds do not. Keep this in mind, particularly, if you're not inclined to do the necessary coat maintenance chores.

- **How much shedding can you tolerate?** If you want a large dog that's *not* a shedder, consider boxers, rottweilers, mastiffs, and the like. Close-coated dogs don't drop as much hair as the fuller coats.

- **How do you like your doggy ears?** Ears go up and ears go down. Which do you prefer?

- **Will you show your dog in conformation, obedience or sport?** Or is this pack pet solely intended to be a companion and family member?

- **Do you want a purebred dog?** If you do, check out the health issues that beset particular breeds. Some dogs need more health maintenance than others, and therefore, impose greater financial obligations.

Dogs are one of life's greatest pleasures, so take enough time to determine which ones are best for you. If you get a puppy, be ready to deal with all those puppy issues, from housebreaking to basic obedience, socialization, chewing, and so on. Raising puppies requires patience and considerable effort. However, on the plus side, a puppy is a blank slate, and you will be the one imprinting on its mind and character. Puppy mischief takes a good couple of years to level off as pups mature. Persistent training efforts will ensure true happiness for many years to come. All pups are wonderful creatures. It's what we do with them, how we train them, and how we treat them that makes them what they'll be for life, and forges their futures and ours.

Getting Another Dog

People tend to choose the same breed or type of mutt the second and third time around. That way, you can be pretty sure of what kind of dog you'll be dealing with. Breed characteristics vary from one individual to another, but the essential type is set, so you know what you're getting. When you choose a mutt, you don't know much about its type. Even though mutts make such delicious pets, some pack parents just prefer the security of picking new dogs of the same breed.

Dogs seem to have a sense of affinity within their own breeds. My own German shepherds seemed to relate best to other shepherds, although their strong herding instinct gave them a nurturing attitude toward all little dogs and puppies. If you have experience with a particular breed, you know its health and exercise requirements. For example, an English bulldog needs much less outdoor exercise than a Doberman or rottweiler. Beagles and bassets are little hunters, far less likely to stay close to you than female German shepherds, for instance. Some pack parents feel more confidence in dealing with their dogs because they know the breed so well, and similar needs can be more readily tended to together.

To be sure, some people get a charge out of having a Great Dane and Chihuahua side by side in the pack. They find the contrast amusing, especially when walking them in public. For me, the balance of three similar-sized German shepherds made more sense. The appropriate pack for you is the one you like best.

Dog clubs and canine shows are great places to see performances by pets and people doing routines that have been honed to perfection. Even if you never plan to show a dog yourself, there's an unbelievable reservoir of inspiration and knowledge waiting for you in these places where pet lovers gather. Novice owners can ask questions of the experts and learn a great deal. But ultimately, it's all up to you: which dogs you'll own, how many, how your dogs will behave, and what you will allow. Keep in mind the rights of others living around you and then have the time of your life with your pack. It's your own sacred journey.

You might as well know in advance that when you get another canine, plenty of other people will become observers of your doggie lifestyle. Some will stay quiet and refrain from offering their two cents, comments, and suggestions, but others, wanted or not, will be eager to impress you with their opinions on the matter. Usually, it doesn't hurt to listen and to learn. Take a lesson from your dogs. They don't mind how much people talk. They wag their tails and go their own way.

The miracle of dogs is infectious. Doggie magic fuels the impulse to increase your canine family and it's oh-so-difficult to resist, especially if all went well with Original Pup. If you're only now on the verge of another dog, let me caution you. A pack of two is *one* kind of lifestyle, but a pack of three, four, or more is a totally different experience.

Preparation

With one dog, it's relatively easy to enjoy canine companionship, whether you're working, playing, or just hanging out. To introduce a new dog into this already comfortable alliance requires a bit of skill and at least a rudimentary understanding of canines. Your first dog should already have a crate. A dog crate is a safe, secure place, a haven in which the dog can comfortably spread out, stand up, turn around, sit, or lie down, where it can enjoy a meal or a good bone undisturbed. Dogs love their crates, and in a multi-dog family, they will readily return to their own crates over and over again, whether on command or at their own behest. Some dogs become territorial about their favorite nesting places.

Crating dogs usually helps improve behavior. Half an hour in the crate is a good period of settle-down quiet time for dogs. They come out of their crates with a much clearer head, ready to work or play. When you remove dogs from crates, first provide an opportunity for them to relieve themselves outdoors. Immediately do a few obedience routines, and then allow freedom to play. You will find that crating creates a much more compliant attitude in your pack. Just be sure you don't overdo crate use or put dogs away for hours of boredom in their crates. I usually provide a bone, a couple of toys, radio music, and a few ice cubes in a dish if I want to leave them crated for more than an hour.

It is not cruel to crate your dogs! It becomes cruel only if dogs are crated as punishment, if they are left locked away for

excessively long periods all the time, or if the crates are put so
far away from everybody else in the family that your dogs languish from loneliness. If you need to leave your dogs crated for
a long time (and a couple of hours is very long for a young
animal) be sure to provide plenty of vigorous exercise beforehand. Before you get a second dog, get a second crate; and
install it in your home before the newcomer arrives. Do the
same thing for each new dog added to the pack.

Dogs do not like sharing their beloved crates, especially
with a newcomer. Older dogs will not take lightly a crate intru-
sion by a newcomer or a guest. Every newcomer to the pack
should have its own crate from day one. Individual crates make
dogs feel safe and secure.

The proper way to acclimate dogs to being crated is to first
provide opportunity for adequate exercise and elimination.
After the dogs have played themselves out and appear satisfied
and ready to rest, say "Go to your crates now," and put them
into their crates. Leave ice cubes in a bowl inside the crate, so
that as they melt, the dog can lick them and the water they provide. Ice cubes will keep them from tanking up by drinking too
much and needing to void immediately again. This consideration is especially important for pups and young dogs. A radio
or television provides music or voices that help crated dogs feel
better and restful. A favorite toy or two should always be available inside dog crates. Most dogs enjoy their crates the same
way youngsters love having a room of their own.

Gradually, by degrees, teach the pack to accept being
crated. Do this with each dog a little bit at a time, always providing happy experiences, toys, food, music, friendly voices,
and release. Lengthen in-crate sessions gradually, and your
dogs will soon become able to tolerate and even delight in
longer periods in their crates. I guarantee that the prudent use

of dog crates will become an invaluable tool in establishing, restoring, and maintaining a peaceful pack environment. If this doesn't work for you, it's probably because you expect your pack to remain crated too frequently or for too long a period. Reduce both and start over again.

Each crate must be large enough to accommodate the *whole* dog, grown into the fullness of its adult body. Wire crates work best because the dogs can see what's going on around them and be part of their environment, even though they're not free to roam. Plastic airline crates block too much of the inmate's view and easily become hot and stuffy, making the animals uncomfortable. Crate pads or folded old blankets covered with an old sheet should be used. Keep them clean and fresh. I had a dog that loved clean sheets so much that whenever I changed my bed linen, he would pull back my comforter with his paws and creep into my bed. I learned to satisfy this canine aristocrat by frequently providing clean sheets wrapped around his crate pad.

When dogs get too rambunctious, lead them to their crates, or send them there if they understand the command. From their earliest puppy days, I always feed my dogs in their individual crates and send them back there for canine time-outs when necessary. Feeding in the crate helps dogs avoid food-grabbing wars and helps instill a sense of security for each member of the pack.

Where to Introduce the New Dog

It's best to introduce dogs to one another in a neutral setting, such as a park or beach, as long as it's safe and not too distracting. This eliminates any territorial issues. Let the dogs get acquainted by sniffing and jostling as they naturally do. Allow them enough time to run and play freely until they tire, by which time they've usually completely accepted each other. Then go home.

If you need assistance, ask a friend to help you. Meet in the prearranged place, each of you accompanying one of the dogs. If you have several to introduce, the more casual you make the encounter, the better. It doesn't matter who gets there first or if you both arrive at the same time—the site itself is completely open and neutral, and that's what counts. The important thing is to let them romp, sniff, and play until they are familiar and comfortable. Having two handlers helps if human intervention becomes necessary, but it usually doesn't. If you have a vehicle outfitted with crates, put the family dogs in first and then go get the newcomer. Put the newcomer into another crate in the same vehicle. By the time you reach your destination, sniffing is well underway already. Let the best-behaved dog in your pack get out first with the newcomer. Release them one at a time until everybody is playing freely. I've never found this to be difficult.

If circumstances make it necessary to introduce dogs at home, such as when you acquire a new puppy, proceed casually and calmly. The family pack waits at home, and you arrive with the newcomer. Show by your demeanor that it's no big deal. Give them time to sniff and examine the newcomer. It helps if you talk quietly in an upbeat and happy voice to encourage them. Puppies are naturally friendly and outgoing so mature dogs, especially females, ordinarily respond well to pups. Even older males generally accept young dogs quite easily into the pack.

Every pup I have ever brought home seemed to awaken parental instincts in all my older dogs. Both male and female licked and sniffed the new arrival, accepting it immediately.

The introduction phase of pack life is not as difficult as it might seem to a novice dog owner, and most multi-dog homes go through this phase quickly and easily. Dogs take things in stride; we should, too.

Introducing a Puppy

As mentioned above, it's easy to introduce a new puppy into the pack. For a few pointers, follow this step-by-step guide:

1. Leave the older dog(s) at home while you go get the puppy.

2. If you prefer to make the introductions at an outdoor site, ask a friend to carry the puppy to that spot for you. Take your dog(s) there and let them approach your friend holding the puppy. If the puppy is waiting in a crate, allow your dog(s) to go and sniff the crate.

3. If you brought your puppy home in a carrier, put it down so everyone can sniff away. After a short period of sniffing, open the carrier door and let the puppy emerge at will. If the older dog(s) growl or appear unfriendly, calm them quietly and reassure them and the puppy before progressing further. If the situation calls for it, remove one or more older dogs and do the introductions one at a time. Since dogs respond to the tone of our voices and read our body language, keep your behavior positive and playful. Say something like this: "Hey, guy(s), here's your new little brother. Good boy. Say hello to Puppy Little."

4. Give plenty of attention to the original pet(s), even if you're holding the new puppy in your arms. Keep a very young puppy in one arm while you put your other arm around the older dog, all the while speaking calmly in a happy, nonthreatening voice. Once the pup is safely placed on the floor or the ground, let it sniff and explore the surroundings. Often, the rest of the pack will follow the youngster and keep on sniffing or nudging it gently. Continue talking to the dogs, petting and reassuring them. The steady flow of your voice is a calming influence to the pack and the newcomer.

5. Giving the puppy its name and introducing it by name seems to make it easier for the older dogs. It's always been my experience when introducing young animals to my pack (puppies or kittens), that all my dogs, male and female, show parental interest right away. They sniff, lick, and explore the newcomer, also allowing it to do the same to them. Dogs that are raised with firmness and affection know what is expected of them and usually do us proud.

Very soon, you'll delight in finding that your older canine will happily lead you straight to the puppy when you ask, "Where's the puppy?" and refer to it by name. Instinct kicks in with surprising rapidity, so don't worry.

Puppies smell good. Mature dogs recognize prepubescent youngsters and readily accept them. Older pups, as long as they don't annoy the pack with obnoxious pestering, are generally accepted without incident. Pet introductions succeed best when all the dogs have been well-exercised and are calm and relaxed.

No matter how well your pack accepts the newcomer, *never* leave a tiny pup alone with an older dog(s). *Never*. Supervision is essential. Whenever you leave the house, crate your puppy and the older dogs, too, until the whole pack is acclimated and adjusted. This could take anywhere from several days to a month. Later, you can leave your older dogs free, but keep the puppy crated whenever you are absent. In fact, crate all new dogs until they are totally part of the pack. It will feel safer for them and all will be more relaxed.

Size alone is prohibitive in large breeds because rough play can cause serious injury to a younger, smaller dog. Stay alert and watchful at all times, but particularly when new members have come into the pack, especially young ones. Older dogs might play very well with youngsters while you are present, but anything can happen in your absence. The very excitement of playing might lead to so much exuberance that an accident could happen. The result would be devastating. Set up the routine early on so that when you're absent, the pack is crated, except for the oldest dogs, that might be exempt.

Sometimes our best efforts fail. I work in Manhattan, a forty-minute subway ride from my Brooklyn home. When Abby first joined our family, I put a baby gate on the bedroom doorway and left my new pup in the bedroom with her toys, food, and water, as well as a newspapered area should nature call. The older dogs had free run of the apartment except for the bedroom. To my surprise, when Abby was only nine weeks old (having joined our family at five weeks), she somehow managed in my absence to climb over the baby gate and join the pack in the living room. When I got home that night, I found all three dogs eagerly awaiting me, sitting together at the apartment door. Despite her successful escape, I knew it would be unwise to leave Abby unsupervised and running free with Grippi and Geisty, who weighed in at 96 and 85 pounds, respectively. So I created a new barrier by adding a few chairs and a higher gate at the doorway of the bedroom. My "Houdini puppy" managed again, despite my best efforts, to leap over the wall and join the big dogs. Day after day, I implemented new and better methods, but they all failed. I finally determined to crate the little Houdini while I was absent, which I should have done from the beginning. From that point on, both of my older dogs stopped meeting me at the door of the apartment. Instead, I would find them nestled against the puppy's crate, keeping watch. There was no reason to fear they would ever harm Abby. Easily and quickly paper-trained, and as my little Houdini was not a chewer, she soon gained her freedom.

Introducing an Older Dog

When introducing an older dog, neutral territory is even more important. First comes the sniffing routine, the dog equivalent to shaking hands. Locked in nose-to-butt formation, they'll circle and sniff for a while. It's possible one of the dogs might attempt to mount another, but this is not a sexual overture. Rather, it is part of the dominance power-play maneuver. The dog being mounted will quickly let the other know this is unacceptable. Watch them, but don't intervene. Body posture reveals whether or not they'll be friends. Follow these steps for a quick and easy meeting:

1. Select a nonterritorial space, neutral for both dogs.

2. Ask a friend to bring the new dog in a separate vehicle.

3. Meander casually toward your friend and the new dog, allowing the dogs to meet unleashed and free. Don't make it a big production.

4. If either dog's tail curls upwards or hackles rise on its back, or if it lifts a lip and snarls, or stands at the ready to attack, intervene quickly and decisively. Use strong verbal warnings and if necessary separate them with a "Cool it, guys." This is usually enough to interrupt the flow of antagonistic energy.

5. If the situation remains uneasy, walk off with each dog and then return to try again.

6. If each has a reasonably sound temperament, several efforts along these lines will usually suffice. For the most part, dogs make friends very quickly. But if they cannot bridge the gap and become more aggressive, you might need to reconsider whether to add this particular newcomer to your pack. I know folks who have to keep their dogs crated separately in three or four different rooms in the house. This just doesn't make sense to me. Why have a pack if it cannot relate? One or two dogs in such cases need to be "recycled" into another living situation. You have to judge whether or not the show of aggression is such that you must stop the introduction. Nobody else can make that decision for you, certainly not in a book.

7. If, after reasonable attempts, you cannot get the pack to accept the new dog, then you should return the animal to its source.

My dogs have always been sound, stable, and well-balanced. In addition, I always provide vigorous physical exercise every day, along with frequent socialization and consistent discipline. Each addition to my pack has proceeded without negative incident. If you have trouble doing this, and you still want to keep the new dog, seek further assistance from a profession handler. In any event, peace of mind and a peaceful pack, not stubbornness, should prevail.

Tougher Introductions

A couple of 100-pound mastiffs, both unaltered males, will provide us with a good example of difficult introduction:

1. Use a safe place, outside in neutral territory.
2. Have an experienced helper assist you.
3. Don't attempt to introduce dogs that are too large for you to handle, even if they don't seem aggressive at first. Introductions can be touchy situations. You should definitely seek professional help to introduce dogs that outweigh and outsize you.

Getting professional help provides a greater likelihood of success. But not every dog trainer has actually dealt with large working dogs. If your helper needs help and asks *you* to decide how to go about introducing the dogs, follow these steps:

1. Select the neutral territory as a meeting site.
2. Go there in separate vehicles, each person with one of the dogs. If you want to introduce your whole pack at that time, take them all along, but let them out of the car individually.
3. Try to arrive simultaneously. If you can't, it's no big deal—the time you arrive will not create a superior position among the animals.
4. If you transport all of the dogs in crates in your vehicle, you and your helper can ride together. When you get there, each of you will take out one dog at a time and give them time to get acquainted. Add another from your pack and then another as the dogs appear ready for more. Don't overpower the newcomer with the whole pack all at once.
5. Take one of your dogs out of the vehicle first and walk off a short distance. Your dog, off leash, will follow you. As you leave the proximity of the vehicle, your helper will release the newcomer, allowing it to run freely.
6. Continue to walk slowly and let the newcomer catch up with you, as it probably will, or turn around and go toward the

vehicle after the newcomer is released. The dogs will run to each other to continue the sniffing ritual begun during transport if they traveled together. When all of them are out of the vehicle running together, give them plenty of playtime so they'll relax. You can judge easily at this point how well the newcomer fits in.

7. Dogs that absolutely refuse to settle down peacefully to romp or run together might be unsuited for pack life together. Make another attempt later, and even a third try after that. If these efforts fail, you'll probably have to return that dog to the breeder or shelter where you got it. You don't want a home where dogs must live separately, crated or by themselves in different rooms. That's not pack life; it's warehousing.

Once the newcomer is accepted, the pack reconstitutes itself, and the alpha dog emerges. This will be either the original alpha or the new dog, whichever one has the most dominant personality. There might be a little roughhousing over it, but this will resolve itself quickly. Remember that male dogs have a go at it and then accept their positions in the pack. It's the females who might harbor a grudge and try to fight it out again later for top dog rank, but females don't challenge male alphas ordinarily. Usually, pack members accept their places at this point, and life goes on. You can see the whole process evolve. When you feel comfortable with it, take them home together.

You've Got Yourself a Pack

After you finish introducing your dogs, they will be ready and eager to move on. New challenges and opportunities await you as pack life continues to unfold. The pack of two you formerly enjoyed is now a pack of three or four. Welcome to your multi-dog home!

By observing the pack, you will soon learn what they need at every moment of the day, whether it's food, exercise, training, rest, quiet time, or fun and games. You'll come to understand the particular aspects of pack life, becoming attuned to their natural rhythms as they become attuned to yours. You're a pack parent now. You're responsible for teaching your dogs everything they need to know for life together—and while you're teaching them, they'll be teaching you! The choreography of pack life is a joyful, happy experience.

With several dogs lying at my feet and a couple of cats perched on my computer, I have written numerous articles and this book, too. My inspiration is the joy of dogs, the happiness of living with the pack. Whatever you do, wherever you go, from now on, you must take into account not one dog, but two, three, or more. Enjoy it!

Chapter 3

Training the Pack

In order to really enjoy a dog, one doesn't merely try
to train him to be semi-human. The point of it is to open
oneself to the possibility of becoming partly a dog.
—Edward Hoagland

Your happiness and success in your multi-dog home is directly proportionate to how well you train your pack. A pack in which every member gets away with doing its own thing is bedlam on four legs. On the other hand are dogs that have been selectively brought together and guided by intelligent training and even-handed discipline. These bond together into a well-behaved pack that respects you as their highest alpha. They are a joy to live with.

Obedient dogs need not be subservient, tails-between-their-legs, fearful, or hangdog in manner. They're peaceful and content because they know the rules and understand what's expected of them. Owning well-trained obedient dogs eliminates risks and surprises. Dogs with good temperament want to please the one who leads and feeds them. That's the one they love. Their loyalty and devotion are unsurpassed in terms of friend or family.

The pack mentality comes naturally to dogs, whose historic survival in the wild depended upon it. The pack mentality will serve you equally well in keeping the pack under control. Pack cohesiveness is a fundamental principle that underpins successful training in a multi-dog household. You are top dog in their eyes. You must establish yourself as alpha with every dog you own. Beside the fact that you control the food they eat, the respect of your pack is built on the consistency and fairness of your demands and the way in which you enforce the reasonable discipline you require. Unless you establish your authority as alpha, it is very unlikely that you will enjoy pack life. If your dogs don't respect you, they'll run you ragged, ignore your commands, and take advantage. Pack life is not for the timid or faint of heart!

Consistency: Don't Change the Rules

Many years ago, my friend Nancy Bekaert inspired me to create my own multi-dog home. I met Nancy at our local Schutzhund club, where we were both training our German shepherds. We later got together with our dogs, and I met the rest of Nancy's canine family. I admired her exquisite control of her pack, four or five canines off leash and obedient. Nancy said that for her, the basic premise for success in living with dogs is "Don't change the rules."

Dogs learn by doing. Once they accustom themselves to the rules we set, it is confusing and unfair to change them at will. Nature's alpha dog is not an on-again, off-again fellow. If your dogs are not allowed on the furniture, for example, that rule must be solid and enforced *all* the time, not just when you're in a bad mood or have company. Once you decide that a particular rule is necessary in your multi-dog home, be consistent about it and avoid favoritism. Waffling damages the respect your pack has for you; inconsistency confuses dogs and chips away at the fundamental regard the human alpha needs to lead the pack. Benevolence and consistency go hand in hand, and dogs return them in kind with their respect and devotion. As you strive to practice these qualities, you'll improve your own character. This is another gift of pack life.

Dogs are quick to notice favoritism in the pack. Playing favorites in pack life is profoundly inconsistent because the rules don't seem to apply universally. Don't let some be permitted such things as cavorting on your bed while others, because of size or tendency to shed, are not allowed. Although dogs can't express it in words, they do feel the hurt of being left out. You might not think so, but favoritism is very detrimental to happiness in the pack. Treat all of your dogs the same, just as you would your children.

Getting Started with Training

Since this is not a training manual, I will limit myself to several suggestions and recommend that you read one or two good training manuals. (The appendix to this book lists a number of excellent training resources.) Historically, most training procedures were harsh and punishing, but today, the best dog trainers prefer kind, motivational techniques. Whether you train your pack yourself or take them to a professional trainer, be sure to use a kind, compassionate approach. I've often heard there's nothing two dog trainers agree about better than criticizing the deficiencies of a third!

Everybody wants good results: well-behaved canines that can be properly controlled and are joyfully obedient. Patient perseverance will get you there. Be upbeat and energetic, accent the positive, and give rewards. Use plenty of praise. Make necessary corrections timely and quick; then, get on with the training. Don't nag, pull, or intimidate. Dogs learn to do by doing, so help them accomplish their tasks, and give them plenty of praise. If the pack happens to do the right thing by chance without a command, use the opportunity to teach them. By attaching the praise ("Good dogs!") to the word describing the desired action ("Good dogs! Stay!"), you'll imprint on the pack exactly what you want. Keep in mind that whether you're training a single dog or working with the pack, the technique is essentially the same. I always trained my two or three German shepherds together and loved it.

Don't engage trainers you don't know unless you first check them out thoroughly. Heavy-handed, punishment-oriented professionals should not be entrusted with working dogs, let alone family pets. Ask to watch a trainer at work before you sign on. Training classes make great learning experiences because watching others is important in the educational process, both for you and your dogs.

Never leave your dogs with someone else for training unless you intend to spend time there learning the same techniques the trainer uses. Otherwise, you'll still be your old regular self when the dogs get back home, and the pack will automatically revert to old habits. Dogs probably think, "Oh, that was just what *that* guy wanted. Mommy doesn't care." You'll be back at square one (minus the money spent on training school). The best trainers teach owners how to handle their dogs correctly. It's like the old saying: If you give a man a fish, you feed him for today, but if you teach him *how* to fish, you feed him for a lifetime. Every day, put the pack through basic obedience routines. Take a few moments to review the fundamentals of come, sit, down, stay. Keep it short, and do it often.

On- and Off-Leash Training

Leashes and collars are not torture weapons. They are tools of the trade. For puppies and small dogs, a round buckle collar or a harness works fine. For larger dogs, once they reach about five months of age, the prong collar is best. Used correctly, this is not a cruel device. It gives a quick pinch to alert the wearer that something is required. I prefer the prong collar to the choke chain, which can cause serious injury. To test them for yourself, put a choke chain around one thigh and a prong collar on the other. Jerk each one hard and release it quickly. Feel for yourself the difference between the prong's quick pinch and the choke chain's pressure. Always make the jerking action short and release immediately. *Do not pull your dogs.*

Leashes should be four to six feet long, no longer. Dogs will try to drag you a million miles an hour unless you teach them how to walk properly on lead. If you train them correctly, walking the pack is really enjoyable and a thing of beauty to behold.

Some multi-dog owners prefer to walk each of their dogs separately, but I love walking my pack all together like a team. They are well-known throughout my neighborhood. On the sad day when one of my older dogs died and my pack was diminished, strangers came outdoors on their porches and greeted me, saying, "You always had three dogs. What happened?" Their sympathy amazed me because it never occurred to me that so many people observed our treks through the neighborhood. People actually said, "Oh, my dear, you must get another dog! We are so used to seeing you with three!"

Dogs that have learned to walk properly on leash quickly adjust to off-leash obedience in situations in which it is safe for them to do so. To prepare the pack, continue basic leash training and obedience. Then take it a step further, to off-leash work. Here are a few tips to help you make the transition:

1. Using food treats, encourage the pack to walk in the heel position near your left side. Keep in mind that even though we call this the heel position, it's not really heeling per se (which is show ring obedience, unnecessary in daily life). Say, "Let's go" instead of "Heel."

2. Call the pack to a proper sit in front of you by holding food treats just below your waist and saying "Here, guys. Come." When they reach you, get them to sit correctly by holding the treats slightly over their heads and saying, "Sit." As soon as they *begin* to lower their butts to the ground, give each a tiny tidbit with praise.

3. The same process works for the "down" and "stay" exercise. Lower the treat hand to the ground and say, "Down." Give the treat with praise. Then, move a short distance away from them. Continue to face them as you walk backward to lengthen the distance. Stand for a while looking their way. When they become proficient at staying in a down position, turn around and walk ten, twenty, or forty paces keeping your back to the pack. Complete the down-stay exercise by calling your dogs giving them their treats, or returning to stand beside them before giving the release command, "Free."

4. Frequent short training episodes improve proficiency. When the pack is reliably trained on leash, you can begin off-leash work, but do this only in a safe location far away from traffic. Follow the first three steps above with your dogs off their leads. If necessary, revert to on-leash work for awhile, and then try off-leash exercises again. Eventually, you'll have beautiful pack choreography!

Fortunately, fundamental obedience work can be accomplished at home right in your own living room. Work through the basic commands described above, and give the pack rewards and praise. Teach them in frequent mini-sessions any time of the day or night. I often review basic training or brush my pack during television commercials. My pack is used to the routine. They have adapted to my standing up to go through their routine while the television chatters away with one sales pitch after another.

Finally, never leave your dogs in a vehicle with leashes attached, even while you're driving the car. Leashes can easily become tangled or caught and injure the dogs. Don't tie them on a porch or near stairways where they can fall off and hang themselves. Don't allow your pack to drag their leashes into an elevator. Pick the leashes up and carry them securely lest they get caught in the elevator's closing doors. Never allow dogs to run with great force to the end of their leashes because the impact on their throats can be deadly. If you must leave your dogs for a few moments to go into a store, don't tie them to parking meters near the curb where cars can inadvertently back into them.

There's no safer way to keep dogs outdoors in the city than by the correct use of collars and leashes. Even suburbs often have treacherous traffic, so don't leave dogs free to roam your yard. Some municipalities make dog trails available in public parks, but in most places, outdoor activities require collars and leashes. Always remove collars and leashes when your pack is at home, and never leave dogs outside unattended.

Noise Control

As social beings, dogs can be very vocal. Most canine sounds are agreeable as long as they're not too frequent, too long, or too loud. Such barking disturbs others and cannot be tolerated. A multi-dog home is not the same thing as a kennel, where barking almost never stops.

Don't let your pack play too vigorously at home, particularly if you're an apartment dweller. Dogs need lots of exercise. If you can't provide regular outdoor activity, maybe you shouldn't have dogs. Without stifling the pack, what is to be done?

When dogs are young, start them off praising and rewarding them whenever they cease barking. The simple word, "Enough," said in a strong voice, usually stops pups from continuing to vocalize. Many dogs are smart enough to learn the difference between full-voiced barking, growling, speaking, and whispering. You can teach the pack to lower their voices.

My first dog was a beautiful German shepherd named Natasha. I easily taught her to bark on command and, later on, to whisper. Natasha loved liver, so every liver treat followed her response to the words: "Natasha, speak." She could not indulge until she made the right sound, which at first was any sound. After she learned to speak on command, I held back the liver until she lowered her voice when commanded to whisper.

Pack behavior is infectious. Training dogs to bark or stop barking on command is not only useful but necessary. Dogs *should* alert us when strangers approach our homes, but they shouldn't serenade visitors during the entire visit! Here's a case in point. My friend owned two Labrador retrievers adopted from a local pound. She loved them dearly but found it intolerable that they barked from the moment guests arrived until they departed. To stop this unwanted behavior, my friend would holler at the dogs in a piercing voice, "All dogs, down!" She continued to scold them loudly while she held dog biscuits over their heads to attract their attention. When the biscuits went up, so did the dogs, jumping into orbit and barking even more excitedly in their eagerness for the treats. The more they barked and jumped, the more my friend yelled, "All dogs, down!" Finally, she grew tired of it all and gave them their treats anyway. I don't know how long it took them to learn this maneuver, but clearly, my friend reinforced it with every guest.

A battery-operated noise-control device is useful. It automatically responds to barking by emitting a high-pitched sound that people cannot hear but dogs find most unpleasant. Unfortunately, if you have a pack of dogs and only one is barking, the others must put up with the unpleasant sound made by the noise-control device until the barker stops.

Some dogs bark from anxiety when owners leave them. If you must leave your dogs alone, as most working folk do, it's necessary to acclimate them gradually to accept your absence without whining, yodeling, or barking. Pack life seems to reduce separation anxiety for some, although most dogs do miss their owners when they are left behind. Try the following steps to help your pack overcome their separation anxiety:

1. Prepare yourself to leave home. Dogs recognize what you're doing when you don your hat and coat. Some of them will flip right into anxiety mode as soon as you start getting ready to go out.

2. Give each dog a treat just before you leave, something that can be quickly eaten so they won't fight over it after you go. If you wish, give another treat when you return, but keep goodbyes and greetings casual and matter of fact.

3. Say something like, "I'll be back soon. Wait here and take care of the house," or simply "Stay." Leave without commotion.

4. Go out the door, and close it behind you. Lock it. Dogs recognize every step in our routines, and they know the sound of the key turning in the lock. They'll know you're only playing if you don't do the exercise exactly like you do the real thing. In the beginning, only stay away a few minutes. If barking persists, return and correct them firmly. "No barking. Stay. Be quiet." Close the door, and start the countdown again.

5. After a few minutes, return and greet them casually. If you engage in a frenzied greeting or tearful goodbye, it just makes it all the more difficult for dogs to remain calm when you come and go. Keep departures and arrivals free from stress, and the noise problem will gradually desist.

6. Go about your ordinary business when you're back in the house. The low-key greeting followed by normal behavior teaches them that you will come and go at will and it's no big deal. The anxiety generated by your departure gradually diminishes as the pack realizes that you must leave but will always return.

7. Repeat the first six steps, above, every few days, gradually increasing the length of time you're away. The pack will get used to your absence, and stress barking will cease. Never leave them free until you are sure they're trustworthy on their own. Prior to that, always crate them when you leave.

What About the Neighbors?

No matter how much we love our dogs, there are times when having dogs is a difficult challenge. This is not because the dogs are a problem, but because the neighbors are!

Some people can't stand kids, cats, or dogs. They come into our lives like bad weather, and there's not a lot we can do to avoid their nasty looks or hostile words. Neighbors like this are frustrating and difficult. The best way to deal with such folks is to keep your pack out of their way as much as possible. For years, I used the service entrance of my building and always put my dogs in a down-stay while we waited for the elevator a good distance away from it.

Generally, people don't hate or fear dogs. If your pack is well-disciplined and reasonably well-behaved, not too noisy or aggressive, eventually, your neighbors will realize there's nothing to get all excited over. In the meantime, hang in there, and don't let it be your fault by ever antagonizing neighbors deliberately.

I have found most people to be fair-minded and reasonably tolerant of my pack. A few pleasant words of greeting maintain friendliness and mutual respect. Keep your dogs close to your body with their leashes held near your thigh so the others can pass without being jostled. If they wish to greet your dogs, as many do, that's fine, but don't expect it. Control your pack by talking as people approach or withdraw. Gradually let out the leashes and give the dogs more freedom after the neighbors have gone.

Responsible dog owners prevent their charges from becoming a nuisance. Clean up after each of your dogs eliminates on the street. Everything depends on how you handle the pack and your own attitude toward the people you encounter, friendly or not. If a momentary failure annoys your neighbor, don't be too proud to apologize and assure the individual that you'll do everything in your power to prevent problems in the future. Good will goes a long way toward helping everyone, dog folk or not.

Street Manners for Dogs That Walk Together

When you walk your pack on the street, expect distractions that might affect their behavior. Train them from the beginning to walk calmly together. Keep your eyes on the dogs and on traffic. Avoid pedestrians, especially the elderly or people with babies in strollers. I put my dogs in a down-stay when people approach or walked around them, leaving plenty of girth. Especially if you have large dogs, be aware that your pack might be quite intimidating. Think and act preventively.

Most dogs, especially young ones, love to meet people.

They'll wag their tails energetically when strangers draw near. You can welcome strangers who want to greet the pack and allow them to pet the dogs if they wish.

Introducing Children and other Dogs to the Pack

When children approach the pack, be mindful that dogs perceive kids differently than adults. Children have jerking, waving, fluttering movements and high shrill voices, which might make dogs defensive even though they want to play. Youngsters can be thrown off balance by the nuzzling of a gentle giant, so, be watchful and attentive when they are near.

Kids are drawn to puppies and even to larger dogs. They love to touch and pet them, eager to see them sit on command or shake hands. If your pack is friendly, greeting children on the street is fun and educational for the kids. But if the pack is not good with children, get them out of the way immediately. Cross the street, or tell the kids to keep going. Don't take risks.

Youngsters always ask me, "Do they bite?" to which I respond, "Only when they're eating."

Recently, a gang of kids descended upon my dogs and me. "Are they friendly?" they chorused. I was tired and didn't want to stop and deal with children at that moment. I just didn't have the energy.

"Yup," I answered. "The dogs are friendly, but I'm not. Keep walking." If you tell the neighborhood kids that your dogs bite, they'll spread that error everywhere, so don't jeopardize yourself and the pack.

I've become a sort of Pied Piper with my pack in the neighborhood. My German shepherds and I take long walks, and there's always an entourage of children that want to meet and greet my canines. Whenever possible, I encourage this encounter and linger if time permits. Dogs and kids are good for each other when properly supervised.

When dogs see other canines, they want to meet and greet them, too. If permitted, they'll jump right into the ancient sniffing ritual. Nose to butt, the dance begins. Don't be surprised that your pack is suddenly straining at their leashes and barking at the top of their lungs. It's a doggie thing! This is the time when your control and attention is really important. If both you and the other dog walker are capable handlers, things usually progress smoothly. The packs stop, sniff, and journey on. But unless you're sure of your pack and you know that the oncoming dog walker is also capable of handling the situation, don't become engaged. Go the other way. As for strange dogs and unattended strays, avoid them like the plague. Anything can happen, and you'll have your hands more than full! It's best for dogs to meet in a safe place where there's plenty of room to run free.

Multi-dog owners often have to juggle several things at once, like leashes, laundry or groceries. Three dogs are quite enough, thank you, but even five can be manageable. For years, I used to see the same ardent pack lover every Saturday night on the Lower East Side of Manhattan, an elderly gentleman who walked down Avenue A surrounded by seven or eight bassett hounds. Each on a separate lead, dragging their long ears on the sidewalk, they marched merrily on their way, oblivious to the amusement they provoked all around them. The old man managed his pack just fine, and it was watching him that probably awakened my first yearnings for a pack of my own.

Behavioral Problems in the Pack

Even the best dog handlers sometime run into problems. Dogs act on instinct, and mistakes happen. Your pack might get overexcited or too rowdy and boisterous. Strong words from you usually regain their attention, and you regain your control. Be prepared to take stronger action if necessary. For example, a particular individual's behavioral problem could impact the others. You might need to isolate such a dog from the pack temporarily while you correct the behavior. Crating is the best isolation chamber when you're at home. If you're away from home, put the dog back into your vehicle for time out. Isolation calms them down and restores order. Removing the culprit prevents the problem from escalating. You might have to take the problem dog for additional individual training, either by yourself or a professional.

Aggression is the most serious behavioral problem to deal with. An aggressive pack is very difficult and can become dangerous. If your pack is getting too aggressive, and you realize your control is weakened so that pack management is slipping to a dangerous level, you must take extra strong action to get hold of the situation. Try taking the following steps:

- Give strong verbal corrections, and keep a very controlled facial expression.
- Physically remove the pack members from the site of their aggression.
- Crate them, or take them out of the way altogether.
- Leave them alone and isolated long enough to quiet down.
- Seek professional help from canine counselors if you are not successful in dealing with aggression problems. Do not ignore them.

Vigorous outdoor activity followed by crated rest periods help resolve most pack problems. The more adequate and intelligent stimulation you provide for the pack, the greater your control will be because your dogs won't feel the need to create their own amusements to relieve the stress of boredom. I used to drive an extra forty-five minutes several times a week to get my dogs out of Brooklyn for a good run. You have to solve any behavioral problems if you want to keep your pack.

Facing the Facts

While it's painful to admit one's pack needs more work, if folks suggest your dogs are out of control, you must think seriously about the consequences. Start facing the facts, and do something about it. We get so used to canine behavior when we live with dogs that we can easily fail to notice behaviors that require intervention and correction. Take a good long look at your dogs, and seek the help you need if their conduct leaves something to be desired. Perhaps another pack parent might be willing to help. But never give up on the pack. They're the most loyal friends you'll ever have. They accept you for who you are, for you're their hero. They wait for you when you go away and rejoice on your return. Their day begins and ends with you on their minds. They notice you first, last, and always, where you are and what you're doing. As author Jeffrey Moussaieff Masson said, "Dogs never lie about love." The effort it takes to hone your pack into a well-trained team is time and energy well spent, an investment that never decreases in value. Pack parenting is all about loving your dogs enough to work and play with them, to train and discipline them fairly and consistently. Mistakes of the pack are really our mistakes, yours and mine. Successful pack management is all about partnering with man's best friend.

Chapter 4

Know Your Dogs

Dogs love their friends and bite their enemies,
quite unlike people, who are incapable of pure love and
always have to mix love and hate in their object-relations.
—Sigmund Freud

Some years ago, walking my dogs in Brooklyn, I found myself frequently meeting a robust young man with long blonde hair and the pack of dogs that surrounded him, jaunting eagerly at his side. The largest was a borzoi named Perry. There were two rescued greyhounds and an azawakh imported from North Africa. The man's name was Alan Koppelman, and over time, our dogs and we became good friends. I learned a lot about pack life from Alan before he succumbed to AIDS. His courage and wisdom inspired me, as did his knowledge and great love of dogs.

Alan's concern for pets that must stay home while owners go out to work inspired him to open his Puppy Day Care Center. His ground floor apartment and spacious patio became a home away from home for many Park Slope pups and dogs. Alan and I frequently compared notes about our dogs. On one such occasion, I queried Alan about his expertise in handling five or six dogs at a time.

"What's the secret?" I asked. "How do you manage so smoothly with so many dogs?"

Alan said, "It all depends on one fundamental premise: *Know your dogs.*"

To know your dogs, you must learn about the innate drives that permeate the deepest level of their nature with the goal of ensuring their survival and reproductive continuity.

Besides these most basic instincts, dogs possess unique personalities, temperament, and characters. To manage your pack successfully, you must understand what makes them tick. Learning about instinctual drives will assist you in training your dogs. Purebred dogs and mongrels alike come from genetic combinations that possess these innate drives in varying degrees. Dog breeding is the art of enhancing and preserving desirable characteristics, and a specific breed type, to ensure that they are passed on to future generations. We are all familiar with one of the most beloved traits in canines, that is, the dog's innate ability to bond unconditionally to its person. Other instincts are equally powerful and necessary. Combined, these drives fire the dog's inner engine. They are its inner essence. If you watch your dogs carefully, observing how they act and react, you will see these innate drives at work.

Prey Drive

Prey drive is the instinct to chase an object and take possession. Early on in their lives, dogs demonstrate prey instinct. The amount of prey drive varies among different breeds and individuals within each breed. You can see how much prey drive your puppy has by its everyday behavior. Why is this so important? For one thing, prey drive motivates dogs to work; it's a great training tool. In pack life, understanding prey drive could help you deter fights by giving you the foresight to eliminate the strong competition and instinct that leads two or more dogs to fight over something they want. Dogs with high or low levels of prey drive behave quite differently from one another.

Dogs always act from instinct. They don't conceptualize or strategize as people do. But that doesn't mean they can't figure out how to get what they want. Prey drive is the instinct that makes dogs pursue, overcome, and take control of an object (also called "booty"). After the chase, they bite it hard, hold on to it, and shake it thoroughly. Once a booty object arouses canine interest, the chase is on! Sometimes, the whole pack becomes engaged in running down attractive booty. Dogs will carry their booty about with them, proudly showing off their mastery of it, or dig holes to hide it for later. Prey drive focuses on food, toys, smaller animals, or other moving objects that attract attention.

This list of indicators will help you get an idea of how much prey drive your puppy has:

- Loves to pounce on toys
- Grabs at a rag shaken in front of him or dragged on the ground at his feet
- Stalks and chases moving objects (toys, smaller animals, and so on) and, when the prey is caught, "kills" it by shaking and mauling
- Takes booty object into mouth to maintain control of it and often buries it or otherwise hides it
- Loves to play vigorous games of tug o' war
- Grabs whatever you hold in your hands if you move it about playfully and pounces on something you are obviously trying to get
- Maneuvers to snatch things away and runs off with booty
- Loves digging holes to hide things

The stronger these manifestations of prey instinct, the greater the amount of drive. Working dogs like German shepherds and Dobermans, for example, are usually high in prey drive, and their training is based on it. When you observe your pack doing a lot of ground or air sniffing, they are on the lookout for potential prey. Smell is the best tracking tool, which accounts for dogs having many more olfactory nerves than humans.

Dogs express their prey drive vocally in high-pitched, excited barking as well as in the postures they assume. Watch your puppy stalking, crouched in the grass, front end down low, ready to pounce, breaking into a loud bark or yelp as it springs into action to seize its booty. It is prey drive that lures the family dog into chasing the cat across the living room or climbing up on a kitchen counter to steal an unguarded morsel of food. Why not? That's nature's way.

In pack life, the established alpha gets first choice of the best prey. Conflict arises when more than one dog wants the same object at the same time. To avoid such hassles, never give treats, bones, or toys to one at the exclusion of the others. Things work best in my pack when I provide several similar objects, like a few tennis balls or rawhide chewies. Never put down only one of a kind for the pack, or they'll likely fight over it.

My dog Grip was a large and powerful alpha, but a gentle one. He often managed to get everything away from Geisty and Cara Mia. He took them to his favorite spot and kept the rest under his elbow while he chewed or played with the one he preferred. The others would approach me complaining until I removed their stolen goods from Grip's hoard. Grip never minded this. He just gave me a doggie grin and kept on chewing his favorite toy. It appeared that he was only proving the point of his position in the pack. My youngest female, Abby, at the tender age of ten or eleven weeks, refused to give up her toys. The older dogs respected her warning growl and left her things alone.

Protection trainers use prey instinct to introduce young dogs to the work by building their desire to capture a burlap sack moved back and forth in front of them. After the dogs learn to focus on the sack, they are trained to bite a sleeve designed for bite work. As they continue training, whether for sport or for serious protection work, as for instance with police departments, they are trained to bite a full body suit. Dogs with the right temperament, grounded in obedience, are not made dangerous by this protection training. Properly trained and handled correctly, they are worth thousands of dollars as reliable professionals. They can excel at the sport of Schutzhund, perform serious police work, or be excellent family dogs. However, protection training is not for everybody or for every dog.

Puppies bite as part of their exploration of the world. Teach your puppy not to bite down hard unless you want it to do so as preparation for eventual protection training. Dogs who are learning to bite for work or sport need a full calm grip.

Defense Drive

Defense drive is the instinct for self-preservation and the protection of owner and pack. The defense trigger is the point at which aggression instinct takes over. These are the physical changes you can see in your dog's appearance when defense drive is engaged:

- Raised hackles
- Low tail carriage
- High-pitched bark
- Withdrawal
- Retreat

Once defense drive is triggered, dogs respond with fight or flight. A dog that is about to fight postures first by raising hackles and tail upwards. It may also reconnoiter before lunging at whatever triggered the defense reaction. Flight is the opposite response, characterized by rapid withdrawal, usually with ears down and tail between the legs. The dog cowers and grovels in an attempt to minimize size or may back into a corner to hide.

Prey, defense, and aggression drives must be balanced to ensure the dog's ability to respond correctly to the proper stimuli. Working dogs are specifically bred for this purpose. They can live well in a pack, but there are certain advantages and disadvantages to owning dogs with strong prey, defense, and aggression drives. The opposite is equally true.

Dogs with a low defense threshold, for example, are easily threatened and quick to react, making them difficult to handle. The lower the defense threshold, the more quickly the reactive aggression response is triggered, firing up the inclination to fight or run away. Dogs with a low defense threshold lack self-confidence, and tend to resort quickly to fight or flight responses. If your dogs fit this description, an animal behaviorist could conceivably help you to build up their self-confidence. However, the fact remains that these characteristics are inbred in every individual dog's temperament, so there's not really a whole lot you can do to change a low defense threshold. Dogs that are more laid back absorb threatening situations without becoming very aggressive. They are easier to handle but less useful for protection. By watching the pack, you can assess the differences in each dog's defense trigger. The best dogs possess balanced drives of prey, defense, and aggression.

So how much stress can your pack endure before fighting or running away? How quickly do hackles and tails go up? Which dog is first to assume a defensive posture? Which is most aggressive? What you want are dogs that can calmly assess threatening situations and respond appropriately. If you have this, you are fortunate. If not, there's work to be done to improve the pack, preferably with a professional trainer. Socialization and training will help, but keep in mind that nothing really changes the fundamentals of innate drives. That's why selecting dogs requires careful consideration.

When to Intervene in Your Pack

Sometimes an older dog in the pack causes difficulties for a younger one, as happens when an adult picks on a less mature member of the pack. Observe before you act. See what the other dogs do. Do they attempt to protect the "victim," or do they jump into the fray and attack the weaker member?

Some dog people suggest letting dogs work out their own problems without interfering, but this doesn't mean turning them loose to damage or slaughter each other. Exercise your best judgment. If one dog gets picked on all the time, or if there's a relatively new dog in the pack being threatened by the others, follow your gut reaction about whether or not to intervene and how best to do so. Allow the pack some time to work things out, but pay attention to what's going on. If things get too hot, give a loud and strong verbal command for the pack to cut it out. Physically pull the aggressors away by grabbing their tails and yanking them backward. Be careful not to get bitten in the process. Some trainers suggest dousing the troublemakers with cold water if possible. Crate them until they settle down. Dogs don't hold grudges, but they might pick on an underdog that is always defended by its owner. Ultimately, it's your decision. No book can provide all the answers.

DeFensive Reactions

When dogs feel threatened, they react defensively either by fight or flight, as we've already discussed. Dogs with stronger temperaments are more self-possessed than those with lower defense thresholds. The following sections describe some defensive reactions you might observe in your pack.

Submissive Urination

Submissive urination is an undesirable defense reaction. Nervous dogs often piddle in stressful situations, even minor ones like greeting someone. Submission urination in puppies or new dogs is unlikely to continue throughout adult life and should be ignored. As they become familiar with the pack, sub-mission urination in newcomers usually stops. Encourage your dog with gentle words and be patient. Do not discipline for submission urination.

Crowding

Crowding is a defensive reaction in which dogs that feel threatened seek protection by leaning against the owner's legs or trying to hide behind them. This is flight behavior. If any of your pack crowds you, jolly them along in stressful situations where this behavior occurs. Use a happy, upbeat voice and calm enthusiasm. They will pick up on your attitude and grad-ually overcome their apprehension.

Raised Hackles

Raised hackles and tails are ordinarily signals of defense reaction, but not always. When dogs meet people and other canines, they aren't usually defensive, but some lift their hackles from excitement, rather than fear. If you're not sure what's going on in the pack, look for other signs. It's reasonable to assume most of the time that raised hackles and tails are signs of fear and flight since these automatic reactions make dogs appear larger and more intimidating to perspective enemies. To counteract nervous posturing, encourage your dogs with a happy voice and joyful demeanor.

Belly crawling

It's a heartbreaking sight to see a dog creeping close to the ground as if it wants to be out of sight underground. Such pitiful behavior usually results from abuse or extreme fearfulness, as when dogs have been reprimanded too severely and too often, or struck, kicked, and otherwise badly treated. They approach their owners with fear and trepidation, belly crawling. I hate to see dogs approach anyone in such a state of subservience and broken spirit, manifesting this extreme fear and flight behavior. Dogs are the most forgiving of creatures. Only prolonged abuse makes them mistrust everyone, including their owners. If you have adopted a fearful dog, be aware that it is possible to rebuild the dog's confidence by persistent kindness, patience, and fairness. Don't despair, and *never* mistreat your dogs.

Tucked Tail

Tucked tails also signify fear and apprehension most of the time, in a defensive posture similar to belly crawling. In rare cases, dogs might carry their tails this way and *not* be fearful, just as raised hackles are not always a sign of fear. Dogs that tuck their tails between their legs generally need a lot of encouragement and opportunities to develop self-confidence.

Dogs that are reluctant to approach their own masters and fearful of strangers have usually suffered some kind of injustice or abuse. They might also be hand shy or even fear-biters.

Once these defensive postures become ingrained through repeated negative experiences, it's very difficult to cure them. Be sure to provide your pack with as many positive, happy experiences as often as possible. These are the essential building blocks of doggie self-confidence and joie de vivre.

Defense flight instinct can interfere with a dog's ability to learn the sit-stay, down-stay, and stand-for-examination in obedience training. This is because the dog needs self-confidence to stay in place when owners back off or walk away. Nervous, fidgety dogs are unable to do well in obedience routines, but they can manage quite happily in pack life once the pack accepts them, which it will do despite their limitations. Actually, dogs that are less confident by nature have been known to make good progress in settling down and becoming more self-assured by gleaning a certain measure of confidence from others in the pack. Unfortunately, the flip side of this coin is that such dogs often become too dependent on the pack, and that's a drawback. The calmer the alpha is, the more at ease the pack will be.

When dogs break command and leave the place where they were told to stay, it is not necessarily defense drive kicking in. They might just be getting ahead of command or trying to anticipate. This is not flight behavior. By understanding the individuals in your pack, you'll easily know the difference.

Biting

Dogs with a high flight quotient component in their defense drive tend to bite from fear when they are cornered. They might even lunge in a preemptive attack, anticipating threats that don't even exist. Highly defensive dogs require very careful handling, with lots of practice in different kinds of situations and environments. They need plenty of encouragement and reassurance to disengage their inclination to bite too soon because of extreme defensiveness. Calm handling could help balance what is lacking in insecure dogs, but such a dog could also become a serious liability. Personally, I refuse to own a dog that is inclined to bite first and think later.

Because dogs always react to human emotion, your pack is affected by your emotional state. Their psychological well-being depends on yours. If you resort to severe physical punishment and harsh verbal corrections, your pack's demeanor will tell the tale. To achieve true pack harmony and happy upbeat dogs, don't scream at them, hit, kick, or push them around. Uncontrolled outbursts of human volatility are always destructive. Dogs that live with volatile, uncontrolled people cannot develop into sound, balanced individuals. The demeanor of the pack reveals much about the owner. Regardless of the level of prey, defense, and aggression drives in your dogs, your own behavior and stability will always be reflected in the pack.

If you have the choice, don't get a dog that manifests a high defense flight drive, no matter how good-looking it might be. These dogs are not suitable for pack life, which requires stability and balanced drives. Be faithful to the animals you already have, however, and work with them if they have problems along these lines.

Aggression

Some folks cringe when they hear the word "aggression," but this is actually an essential basic instinct in dogs. The two kinds of aggression are reactive aggression (a response to external stimuli) and social aggression (the natural impulse to dominate in the pack). The following sections describe the difference between the two.

Reactive Aggression

Aggression is an expression of the dog's ability to fight back against threat. Dogs with too much reactive aggression fight unnecessarily. Their responses are out of proportion to external threats. Nervous and easily agitated, they can be troublesome and dangerous. Such dogs must be kept under control at all times and are not good material for pack life. They are just too unstable, and their inappropriate responses can trigger chain reactions in the pack. If properly trained and handled, certain individual dogs with high reactive aggression *can* be good pack members, but this is not a task for amateurs. Dogs with sound nerve do not get out of control as a result of their high reactive aggression instinct. Without it, dogs would never have become the loyal protectors they are, so this is not altogether a negative trait at all. All instinctual drives, remember, are there for a reason, and only the imbalanced ones are detrimental. Dogs' loyal devotion and protective instinct have made them man's best friend for eons.

Reactive aggression is triggered by threats to territorial space as well as by bodily threats. When they growl at the approach of strangers (human or canine), your pack is simply alerting you that their reactive aggression has been triggered by a likely invasion of their turf. Sporting dogs and serious working dogs are bred for their powerful drives and are trained to react properly to all kinds of stimuli. They are taught when and how to bite as well as to let go on command. They must learn the difference between biting in the game and biting in real life. Built for work, such breeds as German shepherds, rottweilers, Dobermans, and pit bulls make great Schutzhund dogs and excellent personal protection and police canines. They are trained to be reliable; therefore, they are not dangerous attack animals, regardless of what the uninformed might think. Training and supervision are effective tools for correctly channeling and controlling instinctual drives. Because I prefer large dogs, I've always been concerned about canine aggression.

I enjoyed participating in the sport of Schutzhund—which includes tracking, obedience, and protection work—for many years, and I learned a great deal about canine drive from Schutzhund trainers. I know many powerful Schutzhund dogs that are also beloved family pets. The sport of Schutzhund began in Germany more than a hundred years ago and is one of the country's most popular family activities, similar to America's love for baseball. There are Schutzhund clubs throughout the world today, and you can learn much from them.

My greatest reservation about Schutzhund involves the impact on the dog. Along with any other dog sport that requires jumping, climbing, and high-intensity activity, such as leaping to bite a sleeve, this one can have seriously damaging effects on a dog's skeletal system and musculature. Although Schutzhund tracking, obedience, and protection training help develop and channel instinctual innate drives, these high-impact sports can have deleterious health consequences.

Social Aggression

Social aggression arises from certain dogs' natural drive for pack dominance. Dogs often fight to determine who's the top dog, but after the fight, most males accept their places in the pack hierarchy. Females will frequently continue social aggression, seeming to need constant renegotiation of their places in the hierarchy of the pack. Perhaps this springs from the female's instinct to protect her young. At any rate, females often display more social aggression than their male counterparts. Although several dogs of any size and type can live successfully and happily in an apartment or house, outbursts of social aggression might intimidate a new pack parent. This need not be so. To contain outbursts of social aggression, separate your dogs when they get edgy. Give the pack plenty of time to run free outdoors. They will benefit from this release of energy, which will help them to get past some social aggression tendencies. Obviously, if the threat of constant fighting is present, you must be very observant and take all necessary precautions. Do not leave potential fighters free and unsupervised. Consult a professional trainer for additional help.

fundamentals of Pack Instinct

Pack parenting gives you many more opportunities to understand dogs than most single-dog owners ever have. Pack instinct is always there and always operative, causing the dogs to bond deeply with one another as well as with their humans and other species in the household. Yes, indeed, dogs *do* bond with cats, and cats themselves, contrary to ordinary misconceptions, bond with one another and with others in their household. My multidog home is made up of canines and felines in a deeply bonded pack. When my dogs return from outdoors, they immediately check on the whereabouts of our two cats. They seek them out, lick them from head to toe, and then get on with their doggie stuff. Other pack owners also report that their dogs appear to consider the household cats part of the pack. Dogs may want to chase *other* cats while outdoors (prey drive), but at home, they pack together, frequently sharing the couch or bed.

Some manifestations of pack instinct include courtship behavior, mounting, sniffing, reproductive activity, and striving for dominance. Hey, folks, they're just like us! We might not go around sniffing, but pack instinct shows up in humans, too. Most living beings thrive best in an environment of community and family.

Canine Personality: Nerve and Resilience

Dogs have individual personalities just like people do. Some are more outgoing and friendly, while others are the quiet type. Certain dogs demand lots of attention, but some are quite content to rest nearby without a great deal of interaction with peers and people. Some learn more quickly. They differ in their eagerness to please humans. In short, dogs are individuals as well as members of the pack.

Two additional personality factors to consider here are *nerve* and *resilience*. These traits, together with prey, defense, and aggression instincts, determine the personality and character of every single one of your dogs. Therefore, they have a strong influence on your pack's character as well.

A dog's nerve depends first of all on its physical nervous system, that is, how impulses are transmitted to the brain and throughout the body. Calm, confident dogs have sound nervous systems. Resilience, on the other hand, is the ability to bounce back from unpleasant experiences without suffering emotional scarring. Taken together, nerve and resilience enable dogs to accept their entire universe without nervousness, flight, whining, or other undesirable reactions. Solid nerve and resilience make pack life much easier. Extreme weak nerve in even a single dog can affect the general quality of pack life, although it is not inconceivable that such a dog could survive in a family of canines.

Dogs with solid nerve and resilience are fantastic. Their very presence is assuring, and wherever they go, they command respect. They make the best companions and reliable working partners, quite the opposite of dogs with weak nerve who cringe, whine, or run away and who are generally undependable because of their lack of resilience. Unsuitable for work and unreliable as pets, these types are undesirable, and responsible breeders do everything possible to eliminate such from their stock.

If it's a shelter dog you want, try to learn what you can from staff members who received it into the shelter. Why was it brought in? Did the original owner have concerns about its temperament? Was it abused? Was it a found stray? Is it shy? Is it fearful? Even though you can help a dog improve, you can't replace traits that are fundamentally flawed. A serious risk in adopting shelter dogs is the likelihood of obtaining dogs with poor temperament or that are damaged beyond repair from past abuse. With effort and perseverance, in many cases, we can create a happy ending. In all cases, we must strive to shape all of our dogs, even those with weak characters if we have them, into loving and joyful companions.

You cannot trace parental bloodlines in a shelter pet. Therefore, because there's no telling what's in the genetics of the dog, you have no way of knowing how strong the dog's nerve is from the get-go. Even a dog with good pedigree could have some genetic throwback resulting in weak nerve and zero resilience. Yet, these factors are absolutely critical for a happy life. At the risk of sounding harsh, I must say that dogs with *extreme* weak nerve and very poor resilience are probably better off put to sleep. They are so handicapped by these deficiencies that they will always be nervous and can become serious liabilities in the pack.

Mutts are wonderful indeed, but the luck of the draw is even more mysterious and unpredictable in them than in a litter of purebred pups. Nevertheless, great dogs are rescued from shelters every day. Their proven worth in all kinds of life circumstances affirms my conviction that in every pack, there should be *at least one* adopted shelter pet!

Pack Life and Individuality

Dogs are usually born in litters, so their lives begin in the pack. Nevertheless, littermates are individuals, too. We can maximize all our training efforts if we start off by getting to know the subtle differences among pack members. Most of the time, a pack moves with such cohesion that it seems like a single entity. However, every dog is really a unique individual. Each has its own need to interact with you, as owner, with the other canines in the pack, and with other human family members. Interaction is essential, and dogs that do not interact well might become targets of aggression by others in the pack. Be sure to provide lots of quality time and human attention to each and every dog in your pack.

An experienced German gentleman who bred and trained dogs for more than half a century told me that it is best to limit oneself to no more than five dogs in order to be sure that each will receive sufficient quality attention. In the rough-and-tumble of pack life, smaller weaker members need not be pampered, but care should be taken to safeguard them from activities that get too rough for their size or bone structure.

Pedigrees and Titles

In all my years with dogs, I have never met one I didn't like, and that's a fact. Every one of them has well deserved my respect and affection. *All* dogs are gifts of nature that enrich our lives. Dogs with impressive pedigrees are not one bit more wonderful than ordinary mutts of mixed breed. It's all a matter of personal choice whether you select purebreds or mongrels for your pack. German shepherds are my lifelong favorites; perhaps you have yours.

So, just what is the perfect dog? Is it a dog from internationally recognized bloodlines of distinction? Is it offspring of one selected best in breed in a famous dog show? Are Westminster winners the only perfect dogs? Are perfect dogs those that have mastered obedience, tracking, protection, and agility routines and that can perform them with flawless elegance in competition, making their owners mighty proud?

What makes a *perfect* dog? It is humans, after all, who determine selective criteria for measuring canine greatness. But the fact is that the most perfect dogs you'll ever need to know are those that share your life right here, right now. Please, don't forget it. The perfect dogs are your companions and best friends, your own pack. So, what is it that makes them so perfect?

With all due respect for the valuable achievement of best in show and all of the other possible titles any dog can attain in its life and travels, it's the heart of the dog, the inner qualities of its nature that counts the most. Pedigree connects to these things insofar as selective breeding can deliberately enhance drive and character. Pedigree permits you to trace the historical background of your pack. You can review the qualities of each dog's lineage and learn more about the inherited makeup you can expect to find in your canines. People prefer purebred dogs because pedigree records help predict canine characteristics. Unfortunately, the value of pedigrees in general is greatly flawed in ways that are often undetectable because of the unconscionable practices of certain breeders who deliberately trump up fraudulent papers. Such practices are an attack on the integrity of the breeding process. If you care about pedigree, be sure to find a reputable, sincere, and honest breeder before you ever buy another dog. Bloodlines are the blueprints of genetic passage. Pedigree tells us what to expect, but life itself is what determines what our dogs will ultimately become. A good dog is a good dog, and every good dog is a *perfect* one. The hybrid vigor that results from outcross breeding can improve purebred dogs and mutts alike. Perhaps that's why mongrels are so healthy and hardy.

Titling a dog is the final step in a series of training accomplishments that hones the canine-human partnership. Not everyone is capable of bringing a dog to this level of achievement. Titles celebrate the working capabilities of dogs and their handlers. If you enjoy dog sports, go for it, but never underestimate the value of your dog even when it fails to achieve the titles you seek. Keep in mind that most of the time, *we* fail, not our dogs.

Don't overestimate the importance of titles in the canine universe. Pay attention to the qualities of the dogs themselves. Titles do in fact indicate important things about dogs, but they are also the result of excellent training and handling, all of which take time and money to do properly. A dog's value does not depend entirely or solely on the titles it possesses, and neither does yours.

Although working your dogs to title them is a very wonderful thing, your life with the pack goes deeper and is far more significant than any title will ever be. The bond you share with this other species is a window to another world, in itself a great and valuable achievement. Dogs are totally incorruptible and sincere. They tell us a lot about ourselves. Titles indicate the quality of your partnership with a dog, but deception is possible here as it is everywhere else.

Some years ago, I watched a Schutzhund tracking trial in Vermont, in which a beautiful German shepherd competed to the highest level of excellence and scored a perfect 100 percent. Later that day, I approached the owner to congratulate her. I came upon her as she was telling a group of friends how mercilessly she had beaten her dog the night before, while they practiced for the tracking trial during a terrible rain storm. She said that she forced her dog to track correctly by hitting it whenever it failed, and while striking it, she kept saying "Good boy, good boy." The next day at trial, when her dog heard the words "Good boy," it remembered the beating of the night before and kept its nose dutifully glued to the trail, afraid of landing another barrage. The dog ran a perfect track, but in my opinion, the woman herself, alleged champion of the day, was a total failure.

There are many dedicated dog people who love their dogs and train them to perfection using only motivational techniques. Their successes speak volumes about the achievement of titles through kind, compassionate work. Dogs are always at our mercy. In each and every circumstance, they must answer to us, but we must also answer to a higher power.

Pedigrees and titles are a matter of personal choice. My pack is always composed of German shepherds, and I *do* care about their bloodlines. In recent years, however, I have taken greater interest in furthering the cause of shelter dogs, rather than emphasizing pedigrees and titles. The best conclusion of any discussion about these things is to encourage readers to adopt shelter dogs, too.

All dogs love the interaction of training with their owners in a positive, upbeat environment. They eagerly anticipate their desired rewards and work hard to gain them. As long as we understand that the pack's true value derives not from paperwork or trophies but from the dogs themselves, we will have the right attitude toward pedigrees and titles. The fact is—and it bears repeating—that a good dog is a good dog, and every good dog is a *perfect* being.

Chapter 5

Keeping the
Pack Healthy

Mankind's true moral test, its fundamental test (which lies deeply buried from view), consists of its attitude toward those who are at its mercy: animals. And in this respect mankind has suffered a fundamental debacle, a debacle so fundamental that all others stem from it.

—Milan Kundera

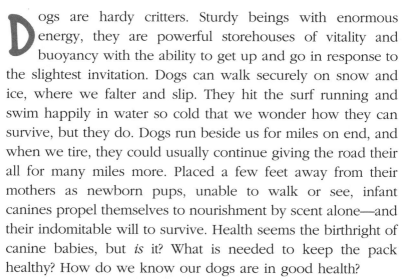

Dogs are hardy critters. Sturdy beings with enormous energy, they are powerful storehouses of vitality and buoyancy with the ability to get up and go in response to the slightest invitation. Dogs can walk securely on snow and ice, where we falter and slip. They hit the surf running and swim happily in water so cold that we wonder how they can survive, but they do. Dogs run beside us for miles on end, and when we tire, they could usually continue giving the road their all for many miles more. Placed a few feet away from their mothers as newborn pups, unable to walk or see, infant canines propel themselves to nourishment by scent alone—and their indomitable will to survive. Health seems the birthright of canine babies, but *is* it? What is needed to keep the pack healthy? How do we know our dogs are in good health?

Dogs can't tell us how they feel. They don't complain about their aches and pains or describe their symptoms when they're out of sorts. It's our responsibility to maintain a vigilant watch over the health of our pack.

Routine Checks

With your multi-dog home, you need to be health-conscious. This is not only because healthy pets are happier and easier to live with, but also because the cost of several dogs with serious health issues can become quite prohibitive. Routine checks reveal the general health of the pack and of each individual. Here's a quick checklist for ascertaining how your dogs probably feel:

• The cool moist nose of a healthy dog is legendary. Nostrils should be clear for breathing and free of mucus discharge.

• Eyes and ears must be clean and clear, as should every orifice, rear and front, and free of discharge or foul odors.

• Healthy teeth meet in a scissors bite, with upper teeth resting slightly out from and above lower teeth. Breath should not smell bad; gums should be pink.

• Heartbeats in healthy dogs are regular and vibrant, easily detected with the palm of your hand pressed against the dog's heart. Panting, the way dogs sweat, indicates heat in the atmosphere or results from vigorous exercise.

• Coats should be vibrant and shiny, with color and markings appropriate for the breed and no bare spots or dried, crusty skin underneath. Skin should be soft and pliable to breathe properly; it should also be lubricated and clean to the touch. (Do not bathe dogs too frequently or you'll dry out their skin. Sponge them down with a wet towel followed by a good brushing to keep them clean.)

• Healthy dogs move efficiently. They glide, prowl, leap, jump, climb, and run with ease and grace, responding quickly from zero movement to high speeds in a matter of seconds, perfectly balanced even while whipping around sharp turns or changing directions. As they age, their natural agility peters out. Just like their owners, most dogs experience arthritis in old age.

• Body fat should be proportionate to size, height, and bone type in healthy dogs that are sufficiently exercised. You can feel a dog's ribs beneath the layer of subcutaneous fat that protects and insulates inner organs. Extreme thinness or obesity shows ill health or even causes it. Avoid excessive treats.

Other signs of poor health are withdrawal, aggression when approached, excessive licking of an affected spot, limping or stiffness, whining or yelping when touched in certain areas, inability to rise from a down position or intense effort necessary to do so, and disinterest or outright refusal to play, run, and jump as usual. One or more of these symptoms suggests the need for a veterinary consultation.

Finding the Right Vet

The services of a good vet are essential for the health of your pack. Whether you prefer a naturopathic and holistic approach or traditional veterinary care, your vet is the third side of the human-canine triangle. Finding the right one is well worth the study and consultation required to do so. Vet care can be quite expensive, too, so try to make a wise investment by getting the best possible.

Ask around for veterinary referrals, and don't presume that every animal clinic is a good one. Pet people are usually glad to recommend vets with whom they are well satisfied. They will also warn you about vets to avoid if they have had unfortunate or unsatisfactory experiences.

The right vet is someone you can talk to about your concerns, who is patient, capable and properly educated. A good vet should be prepared to deliver professional expertise combined with genuine compassionate care, should in short, have a suitable bedside manner, just as humans want for themselves, whether for diagnosis or treatment.

The vet you choose should have a professional environment in which to see you and your dogs. Veterinary office staff should also be professional and courteous. A chaotic waiting room is not a good omen and only increases owner and pet anxiety. If the examination room is not clean, that's a bad sign and indicates the vet is totally unacceptable. Go elsewhere.

Another consideration in selecting a vet is the proximity of the veterinary office to your home or to somewhere you go frequently to exercise your dogs. You will also need to consider how you are going to travel to get there:

- Will you drive to the vet? If yes, is adequate parking available?
- How long is the trip by car?
- If you don't drive, will you use a taxi or hired car?
- Can you get to the vet's office by bus or subway? (In some cities, dogs are permitted on buses or subways, depending on size, breed, and manageability.)
- Is there someone you rely on to take you to the vet?

I know dog owners who travel great distances with their pets to consult veterinarians whom they trust or to obtain specialized services, such as chiropractic care or acupuncture.

Occasionally, there's just not enough time to make a long trip. To be on the safe side, you should compile a list of possible veterinarians who are not too far away, whom you could consult if your needs are too urgent to reach your usual vet or if he or she is on vacation. Post your list of local vets and medical offices, along with addresses and phone numbers, in a readily available place, like on the refrigerator, for example! It's best to use a veterinary practice that offers twenty-four-hour coverage if you can find one, but in any event, back-up is essential.

Choose a veterinarian licensed for the state in which you live who is trained in health issues specific to your breed. Providing health care for your multi-dog home can land you in a real financial mess, so you might want to consider animal health insurance as an option.

Insurance for the Pack

For twenty years or more, pet insurance has been developing and expanding as more owners and veterinarians have become interested in the benefits it can provide. Pet health policies today are much like those designed for humans, with deductibles, co-payments, premiums based on monthly and annual rates, and a variety of coverage plans. The best plans offer coverage for medical, surgical, pharmacological, and dental services. They include provisions for annual checkups, vaccinations, other routine work, and emergency care as well. A definite added plus is coverage for any particular problems relative to your breed.

Besides this, you'll need a plan that covers more than one animal per household. The final decision about getting pet insurance is yours to make, but the promise of providing canine kids with excellent veterinary care—without going broke in the process—necessarily demands that you examine the issue thoroughly. Talk it over with your vet and other pet owners, and do more research before making up your mind.

Dog Behavior in the Vet's office

Taking dogs to the vet is an integral part of pack life. If you've been working on canine manners all along, it will carry over into your dogs' behavior at the vet's office. If you haven't, better start now. Here are some basic rules for humans and dogs at the vet's office:

- Sit still, and avoid unnecessary noise or movement.
- Be polite, and answer the doctor's questions thoroughly.
- Don't interfere with someone else's appointment.
- Be on time, or call ahead if you are going to be late.

Practice good behavior until your dogs are capable of keeping the rules. You can do this in your living room at home several times a week in brief practice sessions. The pack's actual trip to the vet's office begins with loading the car. In the best of circumstances, traveling with dogs requires forethought and patience. Many multi-dog owners use crates in their vehicles to ensure safety, but I prefer my dogs to occupy their own places in the car. This allows them to be protective if necessary, especially in some of New York's dangerous streets or on long road trips into the unknown.

Eliminate as much emotional distress as possible. Dogs feel us out psychically and seem to know they're going to the vet's office, regardless of whether or not we tell them. I like to play the car radio and talk quietly to my pack en route to keep them relaxed. It's a misconception that dogs don't pay attention to what we say. Personal experience shows that agitated dogs often respond well to a calm, reassuring voice. Music is also helpful in soothing upset animals.

On arrival at the veterinary clinic, keep the pack quiet and fully under control in the waiting area and examining room. If the whole gang is too much for you to handle, take one or two dogs in at a time and leave the others in your vehicle (unless it is too hot outdoors to do so). Keeping the pack under control during travel to the vet's office sets the tone for the whole experience. If they're all revved up ahead of time, their exuberance, coupled with anxiety about seeing the doctor, can make office visits difficult.

Keep your dogs on leash going to and coming from the veterinary clinic. Hold the leashes close to your body so the dogs don't get an opportunity to enter the office gangbuster style and disturb others already there waiting their turn. My limit at the vet is three dogs at a time. More power to you if you can manage more! You should also consider the advantage of leaving the pack at home and only taking the dog that actually needs this particular veterinary appointment.

If the veterinary visit is not an emergency, get your dogs out for a good run before going to the clinic. This will take the edge off their energy and anxiety, besides tiring them out so they'll be happy to lie down quietly in the waiting room until the veterinarian is ready to see you.

Vaccinations

To vaccinate or not is a controversial issue with serious implications on each side of the argument. The debate about when, how often, and for which diseases to vaccinate is being debated by animal health care specialists and owners. There are risks and benefits, no matter what you decide.

In the past, people believed that vaccinations were not harmful but healthful. Today, it is widely understood that vaccines introduce toxins into the body which, added to the generalized overuse of antibiotics and poor quality foods, plus those toxins to which dogs are exposed in their daily living environments, produce ill side effects overall. Allergies, organ failures, and other problems result from overvaccinating pets. The vaccinations, themselves, require canine immune systems to work overtime.

When multiple vaccines are introduced simultaneously, as in the "vaccination cocktail" style that was so popular not long ago, dogs are further victimized. Their immune systems become completely overstressed, and instead of getting good results, the opposite occurs. Studies show that multiple vaccine shots, such as the usual combination given to puppies against distemper, hepatitis, leptospirosis, parainfluenza, and parvo, are too much for their young respiratory and gastrointestinal systems to handle.

Furthermore, puppies ingest immunity reserves through their mother's milk anyway, so vaccinations can wait, according to some vets, until pups are about five months old. The fact is that maternal immunity can actually interfere with vaccines given to puppies before eight weeks of age, thus neutralizing the good effects hoped for in the vaccination process. The underdeveloped immune system of young pups can be weakened for life as a result of vaccinations. It makes you stop and think, doesn't it? Unfortunately, not all veterinarians are equally informed about new research in vaccination practices.

For years, conscientious dog breeders have recommended that dogs be given a simple blood test, known as an antibody titre test, to measure the presence of antibodies to specific diseases like distemper and parvo. Increasingly, more veterinarians are endorsing this approach. By having your dogs titred, you can find out if they actually need to be vaccinated or not. That makes more sense to me than racing off to get shots that can prove more harmful than beneficial.

I am not a veterinarian or dog breeder, but having loved dogs and studied these things for a long time, I want to pass along to you the results of my research and encourage your own. I make no claim to answering the dilemma for others. It's your call. Vets have their own protocols for vaccinating dogs, and these often differ from one veterinary practice to another.

A recent report stated that at least twenty-seven different veterinary schools throughout North America are changing their vaccination protocols for dogs and cats. There's abundant material about this online. In addition to consulting with your own vet, personal research is a good idea. (Check the appendix of this book for helpful resources.) Regardless of which side of the vaccination debate you come down on, your dogs and you must live with the consequences.

First Aid for Dogs

Hopefully, you'll never have a major emergency with your pack, but forewarned is forearmed, and rudimentary knowledge sometimes saves lives. The first step toward helping pets in an emergency is to keep them calm, both the injured and the others. If possible, remove healthy members from the scene so you can deal with total attention on the dog that is hurt. Dogs seem to have a mysterious innate ability to comprehend emergency situations to some degree, and their behavior often reflects a primitive understanding we can't quite explain. A few years back, a car hit my dog. After the accident, the rest of my pack and my friend's two other mutts quietly and obediently did exactly what we commanded. They cooperated perfectly, allowing us to focus completely on first aid care for my injured dog until we could get her to the nearest animal clinic.

In an emergency, get experienced veterinary assistance at the nearest location available. There may, however, come a time when your dog's life depends on your ability to administer first aid immediately. Ideally, one would not attempt doggie CPR without expert training beforehand, but in the case of dire emergency, I most certainly would make the attempt rather than allow my dog to perish. A brief discussion of first aid treatment is included here, but you should expand your knowledge by further study.

One situation in which you should take immediate action is if an animal is rendered unconscious and nonresponsive, with halted breathing. To assist a dog with a blocked airway, follow these steps before attempting to administer CPR:

- Check to be sure nothing is obstructing the airway by looking into the mouth and throat for blockage.
- Reach in and remove the foreign object if it is visible. Do *not* attempt CPR unless the airway is clear.
- If blockage is apparent but the object cannot be reached, turn the animal so its back is against your chest. Administer the Heimlich maneuver by squeezing hard with both arms and giving sharp bear hugs to the abdomen of the dog so the object will be expelled.
- When the airway appears clear, with nothing trapped there, move the dog's tongue to the side of its mouth, careful to avoid further injury to the dog or a bite to yourself.
- Straighten the dog's neck so the head will be in reasonable alignment and air passage free and straight. Make the head adjustment carefully, especially if the dog has injured its neck.
- Make sure the dog is not bleeding.
- Make the dog lie on its right side, and close its mouth.
- Use mouth-to-nose respiration at a rate of twenty breaths per minute.
- Compress the chest three times every two seconds.

After every fifteen compressions, give two mouth-to-nose rescue breaths.

- Get the dog to an emergency clinic as soon as possible.

Stay calm and cool-headed. By being centered and peaceful yourself, you'll be able to carry out first aid tasks correctly. Your calmness will be passed on to the injured animal, whereas if you panic, the dog might pick up on your distress and become less manageable. As soon as the dog is breathing again, or even sooner if it appears that your efforts are not going to work, get it to the nearest emergency clinic for complete medical treatment. Remember that ordinarily, only a trained individual who really knows how to give CPR should attempt to do so, but in a dire life-threatening emergency, it's better to make the effort than to lose the dog.

Plants That Poison Dogs

Dogs are great scavengers. Singly and as a pack, they love to search and sniff about, picking up tidbits to nibble and sometimes getting poisoned in the process. Exercise vigilance lest your dogs devour plant substances that are toxic, as some seemingly harmless household plants can be. Not all dangerous plants are included in the list that follows here, and besides, it can happen that individual dogs suffer an unexpected allergic reaction to plants not listed. The topic of plants that poison dogs is by no means comprehensively treated in this book. Toxicity can be a very personalized problem!

Don't keep dangerous plants in proximity to your dogs, but if you must, and if there's reason to believe a member of the pack has found its way into the garden or among poisonous household plants, you must take immediate action. Call the ASPCA's

National Animal Poison Control Center at 1-888-426-4435.

Before such a calamity occurs, you should have already located and made a note of a specific animal poison control center in your geographic area. Have this information available. Check your telephone directory for the number and location closest to you. Be vigilant with your pack. If any one of them ingests harmful plants, go immediately to the nearest veterinary clinic.

Cornell University posts a specific page about poisonous plants on its Web site, at *www.ansci.cornell.edu/plants.* In fact, several universities have similar sites where you can research poisonous plants more fully, such as the Purdue University School of Veterinary Medicine, for example. Awareness of harmful plants is important to pack parents because dogs get into things together. One dog will see something, sniff, and eat, and soon, the others follow! Here is a list of plants that could be very dangerous to your pack:

- Bulbs of the amaryllis, autumn crocus, daffodil, day lily, elephant ears, gladiolus, hyacinth, iris, lily of the valley, narcissus, orange day lily, and tulip
- Vines in the ivy families
- Succulents, like aloe vera
- Flowers and ferns like cyclamen, hydrangea, kalanchoe, poinsettia, emerald fern, and lace fern
- Houseplants like cut-leaf philodendron, cornstalk, devil's ivy, peace lily, taro vine, and marble queen
- Shrubs and trees such as the holly, rhododendron, philodendron, yucca, avocado, and macadamia nut tree

Not every dog that encounters these plants will necessarily die from their toxicity, but caution is the better part of wisdom.

It's important to think about the plant life in your home environment that is accessible to your pack.

Finally, the information in this chapter is not intended to replace your efforts to seek veterinary assistance as needed or to continue broadening your understanding of canine health issues. Apart from ordinary illnesses and accidents that require first aid, in general, you can rely on excellent nutrition, exercise, and rest to sustain your dogs in good health, particularly if they are genetically sound. Because of its importance in the health of the pack, canine nutrition will be considered in a separate chapter.

Chapter 6

The Natural Pack: Herbal, Holistic, and Homeopathic Dog Care

They are not brethren, they are not underlings; they are other nations, caught with ourselves in the net of life and time, fellow prisoners of the splendor and travail of the earth.
—Henry Beston, *The Outermost House: A Year of Life on the Great Beach of Cape Cod*

I t's incomplete to talk about canine health without including a discussion, however brief, of the best natural means to this end, namely herbal, holistic, and homeopathic care. Dogs are one of nature's best ways of making people whole, healthy and happy. Why not, then, give them back, individually and in the pack, the best of nature for their own health and happiness? There's nothing better than nature's best, and the natural dog is just that, purebred or mixed in origin, nature's best. That's why, perhaps, D-O-G is G-O-D spelled backward!

I once heard a delicious anecdote that portrayed the Creator in the Garden of Paradise reviewing all that He had made and seeing it was good, as the Bible says. After the Lord God made the universe, He named everything that was in it except one being. This unnamed creature asked God why He had left it alone unnamed among all the other beasts of His kingdom. Was it to condemn this creature to being forgotten in the annals of the earth? No, far from it.

The Creator pondered the dilemma and reviewed the names of all the beasts of land, sea, and air, wondering what to name this last being, a furry, four-legged animal. Finally, he summoned the unnamed one and said: "You shall be called 'Dog.' I have left you until last so that you may have my name, written in reverse. Of all creatures that walk on four legs, you shall be the most loyal, the most loving, and the most faithful.

You shall be my gift to the earth, cherished by humankind whom I shall create in my own likeness. From now on, you shall be called 'Dog' just as I, the Creator, am called 'God,' and you shall bear my blessings to humankind all over the earth until the end of time."

Okay, so, I doctored it up a little bit, but you get the idea. Not knowing the origin of this delightful tale, I cannot properly give thanks, but I am grateful all the same, that God and Dog have been my life's most faithful companions.

Dogs evolved through eons of time, recorded and beyond. The concept of an "herbal pack" represents a conscious decision to introduce natural health-care products into the management of the multi-dog home. According to Greek tradition, dogs and cats were themselves natural herbalist doctors long before people got involved. They seemed capable of seeking and eating a wide variety of herbs that met their health and nutritional needs in the wilderness or when left to their own devices living among humans. So it seems that the natural dog was an herbalist of sorts.

Although I am not an herbalist, naturopath, or a health researcher—and thus can make no claim to extensive personal experience with herbs or homeopathy—I am very interested in these alternatives and believe them to be key to successful pack health. Nor am I alone in this, for the continuum of holistic, herbal, and homeopathic veterinary care is ever-expanding. This chapter contains only rudimentary information acquired in my long search for understanding more about canine health care. You'll have to pursue this much further on your own, as I, too, intend to do, but I hope this section whets your appetite for learning. The literature indicates a continuing increase in the use of alternative therapies in veterinary medicine. In the final analysis, it's our animals that will enjoy a better quality of life.

What Can Herbs Do for Dogs?

Although medicinal herbs don't taste very good, they can be very effective in therapeutic interventions. Besides healing health problems that are already underway, herbs can deter further problems from developing by helping to address immune deficiencies in animals as well as people. Herbs ease the physical side effects of stress and trauma, reduce fear, and soothe the anxious dog. They relieve inflammation that leads to arthritic stiffness and discomfort. They improve mobility and relieve pain. Some herbs assist in digestion or can be used to supplement your dogs' diets for better nutritional absorption. Herbs can be used safely, working together to build immunity and combat deficiencies.

What makes herbs so useful is the way they trigger the body to heal itself, but since their taste is so unappealing, efforts have been made to improve the delivery system. The extract mode is the best form for administering herbal treatments because extracts enter the bloodstream quickly. One improvement is to put herbal formulas into honey-based products that make herbs palatable. Honey itself is therapeutic, so honey-based herbal tonics have the added efficiency of delivering these natural benefits as well. Honey is an energy-producing, cardiotonic, nerve-enhancing, predigested delivery system. What could be better? Dogs take to it like bees to honey! In addition, honey also possesses sufficient antibacterial properties to make it an immune factor metabolizer. It is also a natural antioxidant. Herbs can be administered in pill or tablet form, as teas, or as oils added to the dogs' meals. They can be made into poultices or compresses that can be applied externally as needed, or as ointments to spread on a wounded area. Don't take it upon yourself to concoct any of these applications.

If you're interested in the power of herbs for treating dogs, consult a qualified animal herbalist practitioner about what to give your pack, how to administer it, how often, and how much. A professional like this will tell you where you can obtain human-grade herbal formulas ensured to be of the best quality for people and pets. When buying herbs, read labels carefully and follow directions exactly. Aging dogs and people can benefit particularly from herbal therapies.

Beneficial Herbs

Briefly, here are some beneficial herbs you will want to learn about for potential use in helping your pack:

- **Flaxseed oil:** Helps to reduce triglycerides and cholesterol that block arteries and cause blood clots. Flaxseed oil is one of the best sources of omega-3 fatty acids. Your pack needs a regular "fix" of flaxseed oil. Give it to them and watch for their clean, sparkling coats.
- **Ginkgo biloba:** An anti-aging herb, has positive effects on heart and nervous system. Has been used successfully to help patients with memory problems and depression, both human and canine, by boosting long-term and short-term memory. It also improves circulation.
- **Gotu kola:** Herb used extensively in Chinese and Ayurvedic medicine, is a strong antioxidant that protects the body from the damage of free radicals and offers relief from stress-induced illnesses and memory loss.
- **Green tea:** Healthful because it contains flavonoids and polyphenols that are even better antioxidants than vitamins C and E.

• **Ground barley, marshmallow root, slippery elm bark, and meadowsweet**: A good mix to which raw honey can be added for an effective therapy against upset stomach, diarrhea, and other intestinal discomforts.

• **Rosemary**: A strong antioxidant, prevents the breakdown of a brain chemical known as acetylcholine, thereby contributing to the delay and prevention of senility. Since dogs also suffer from old-age syndrome, rosemary is good for the pack and people, too.

• **Tumeric**: A yellow-colored antioxidant that contributes to cardiovascular health and the production of bile by the liver.

• **Yucca root, devil's claw root, boswellia, bromelain, and meadowsweet**: An herbal blend that makes a helpful agent against arthritis and joint-related problems in dogs.

All of these herbs (and more besides) will enhance the health potential of your pack, but you must find out from an herbal specialist exactly how to use them correctly and for the greatest benefit to your dogs. It's fascinating to read accounts of dogs with seemingly insurmountable and even terminal health problems that made radical progress when given herbal therapies. The use of herbal remedies in veterinary practice in the United States is very recent, so don't be surprised if your veterinarian is a little slow to catch on. You might have to look around for someone to help you who is really qualified to do so.

Herbal therapy is an interesting topic because it holds out for us the promise of great strides in veterinary care. In France, Germany, and the Netherlands, the market in herbal medicines has expanded at a staggering rate. On this promising horizon, we can hope to see many improvements in available health care alternatives for animals as well as people.

Bach Flower Remedies

The Bach flower remedies were first prepared in the 1930s by a British physician named Edward Bach, who created a mix of five floral remedies that later became known as Rescue Remedy. This substance is highly regarded as a natural reliever of stress in animals and people. The five floral remedies that make up Rescue Remedy are rock rose, Star of Bethlehem, impatiens, cherry plum, and clematis. Many well-known dog experts, breeders, and handlers swear by Rescue Remedy when their packs need a soothing, calming treatment for emotional upheavals of all kinds. Rescue Remedy is good for soothing a dog stressed from being left alone or adapting to new surroundings. It's also good for conditions like shock, mistreatment traumas, the fear of loud noises and storms, and the grief of losing a pack parent or member, car sickness, and kennel anxiety. The Bach flowers help restore balance and harmony in the physical body, and this in turn induces emotional relief. People who use Rescue Remedy to relieve their dogs report positive results. Here are some of the Bach flower remedies:

- **Agrimony** can help to reduce persistent self-mutilation by chewing and scratching in anxious and agitated dogs.
- **Aspen** helps animals that are fearful before or during severe storms, floods, and natural disasters. When you must euthanize an animal in the pack, you might want to treat the others with aspen to lessen their apprehension about the loss of their packmate.
- **Beech** quiets noisy, barking, whining, squawking dogs that are intolerant of things like weather and climatic changes, the presence of other animals, new relationships in the family, or new dynamics in the pack.

- **Centaury** raises the will to live and reduces enfeebling effects of illness or surgery in animals that are very sick.
- **Cherry plum** reduces frenzied and crazed behavior, for example, the panic of dogs in response to intense trauma. It is useful for treating dogs that are on the verge of becoming out of control and dangerous, destructive, or frantic. Cherry plum is also helpful in treating seizures or anxiety attacks, as well as for certain allergies to specific grasses.
- **Chestnut bud** helps cure dogs that chew on shoes and other household items, chase cars, or jump all over people. Chestnut bud is considered an herbal enhancer of awareness.
- **Chicory** is good for demanding pets and overly possessive pack members. Chicory is also helpful against nasal or lung congestion.
- **Clematis and impatiens** increase attention span and the ability to focus. They ease pain and help soothe dogs that are overexcited or upset, as when left behind in a kennel. These are helpful in focusing guard dogs, hunting dogs, and Seeing Eye dogs. Clematis is also used to return an animal to consciousness after being comatose or unconscious.
- **Crab apple** is a cleanser that reduces animal odor and alleviates the unclean feeling associated with infestations of lice, fleas, ticks, or other parasites. Crab apple combats internalized toxins and can be used to cleanse infected wounds or rashes.
- **Rock rose** is used to treat panic and fear. It enhances the animal's innate courage, so it is useful for service dogs or in pack life for dogs prone to panic or fear.
- **Star of Bethlehem** works against all forms of trauma and severe emotional distress. Star of Bethlehem is used to give supportive comfort to animals left behind in a boarding kennel.

Holistic Care

As you learn more about your responsibilities in parenting the pack, you will doubtless come into contact with the expanding role of holistic medicine among vets and people doctors alike. It's well worth your while to learn more about this approach to health care, and that's why I am including this brief but important discussion. The philosophical underpinning of holistic veterinary practice is first to discover and eliminate the causes of illness and pain by trying to determine what makes pack members sick. Then, it aims to decide what can be done to make them better, attacking the problem in a broader scope than traditional practice would. Some methods used in holistic medicine are very ancient but still totally relevant today. The American Veterinary Association approves of these methods, and veterinarians must train for years to implement holistic practices along with conventional care. So what's the difference?

Conventional veterinary medicine is based on the Western paradigm of medical practice in which a diagnosis is determined by means of a physical examination, blood work, x-rays, ultrasound, and urinalysis. Following the diagnosis, medical treatment is administered, including such things as antibiotics, dietary change, surgery, and steroids.

While the traditional Western medical approach to healing disease is often invasive, the holistic approach is not. Holistic medicine is more like an umbrella term that covers four major types of therapy: homeopathy, acupuncture, chiropractic, and herbal medicine. It also includes touch therapy, such as massage, magnetic therapy, and aromatherapy. However, most holistic practitioners are not completely unconventional, generally including traditional Western therapies in their practices.

The combined package of all these methods makes up what is known as holistic medicine.

We are fortunate to live during an era in which holistic medicine is being increasingly understood and widely accepted for animals and people. The holistic approach makes sense because it incorporates the best of all therapeutic modalities that can be applied to any health situation, whether preventative or curative.

Pack problems relating to health respond positively to holistic veterinary care. Some of these include lameness, chronic pain, skin conditions, muscular difficulties, and skeletal issues. Despite the fact that some vets continue to consider alternative treatments as unconventional therapy, they are successful in helping patients suffering from cancer, arthritis, gastrointestinal ailments, and many other human and animal ills.

Acupuncture for Dogs

For centuries throughout Asia and then later, on many other continents, acupuncture and herbal medicine has been successfully practiced by revered medical personnel. It was not considered anything but mainstream medicine. In the West, this wasn't so, but as the population becomes more educated, people are seeking out less invasive cures and more positive preventative treatment.

Your dogs can benefit from acupuncture treatments for many health problems because acupuncture taps into the body's own energy system and helps it to heal itself. Very thin needles are inserted into acupuncture points on the surface of the body, in places that connect to the flow of energy. Finger pressure on the same spots can do the same thing without using needles. Acupuncture practitioners train for many years to master the art of locating and applying acupuncture or acupressure to the body's major pressure points. This is not a quack idea, but a certified historical therapy. Try it and you'll see.

Homeopathic Pack Life

Informed pet owners want to include homeopathy in health treatments for their packs. Homeopathic veterinary care can help dogs (and cats) suffering from minor indispositions or acute illnesses. It takes into account not only the present illness and its symptoms but also the whole of the dog. Homeopathy pays close attention to the physical, mental, and emotional aspects of its life insofar as these can be ascertained. All these factors interact and cause illness. Diagnosis alone is not the whole picture. Each individual's history must be taken into account to prescribe homeopathic therapies.

Homeopathy began in the 1800s. It was based on the work of a German physician named Samuel Hahnemann, who studied conventional medicine first and then examined other kinds of treatments that might be prescribed in specific cases. His studies revealed that these medicines could not only cure people, but kill them as well, because excessive dosages were toxic. Considered to be revolutionary at the time, Dr. Hahnemann's findings said the remedies themselves could add to health problems and even make deteriorating conditions much worse. Hahnemann tested certain remedies on healthy people and proved that the cure could become the cause. He realized that there is much more to treating illness and disease than merely suspending symptoms. Drug therapies mask symptoms without eliminating the essence of a disease. In homeopathy, the symptoms are only the expression of the disease itself, but the cure must go deeper than the symptoms.

Dr. Hahnemann's work paved the way to radical changes in the elimination of disease. Sometimes there is no complete cure, but homeopathic interventions can still make the patient much more comfortable by alleviating the root cause of the illness. Most assuredly, such wisdom can be applied effectively to the health issues of your pack. Homeopathic veterinary care aims at alleviating deeper conditions, whether physical, mental, or emotional, giving the sick animal a larger opportunity for healing. Coupled with holistic treatment and traditional veterinary medicine, homeopathy can add great benefits to restoring health to the pack. Instead of being competitive approaches to healing, these are absolutely complementary. Taken together, they give us a much more complete approach to healing our dogs and ourselves.

As dogs have traveled with people into the twenty-first century, they have not only benefited from advances in technology and human knowledge, but they have also suffered the toxic results of a world in which there are far too many violations of nature. Toxins abound in the foods we eat and those we feed our pets. Drug treatments produce as many deleterious side effects as cures. Our dogs are swept up into progress that is sometimes deleterious to health and, therefore, that is not progressive at all. It's time to look long and hard at the underlying causes of canine illness and death. Nature's pack, entrusted to us when we become multi-dog parents, depends on us for everything. Our job is all about our understanding of the laws of nature and our acceptance of its basic rules. Herbal therapy, holistic medicine, and homeopathy are three facets of the same jewel, a natural approach to the preservation and enhancement of life.

Chapter 7

feeding the Pack: canine Nutrition

Ever consider what they must think of us? I mean, here we come back from a grocery store with the most amazing haul—chicken, pork, half a cow. They must think we're the greatest hunters on earth!

—Anne Tyler

eeding wisely is the best way to ensure the health and longevity of your pack. Did you know that hyperactivity, restlessness, lethargy, inability to learn, aggression, and unruly behavior can sometimes be traced back to poor nutrition? Or that a dog's peculiar skin odor or oily, foul-smelling coat may be due to the high level of toxins it is fighting? Poor nutrition causes many problems, and owners often don't suspect that it's the culprit in issues that involve physical health, emotional and mental stability, neurological function, and behavior. A sound nervous system, essential for good temperament, depends on good nutrition for daily sustenance, growth, repair, and upkeep. Food is the bottom line of all life functions.

Besides fresh water—I suggest you change your pack's water supply twice daily—dogs need enough good quality food to meet their size and energy requirements. Since dogs love to eat, left to their own devices, they'll ingest just about anything imaginable, hungry or not. Parenting the pack responsibly means keeping a commitment to provide the best food possible within reasonable budgetary and time constraints.

Nutritional needs differ depending on breed, age, and size. Pregnant mothers and lactating dams have different requirements than older dogs or dogs with allergies. Some things are very dangerous for dogs of any age or condition.

Never give dogs chocolate. It might be a treat for you, but for dogs it's disastrous. Chocolate contains an ingredient that is completely undigestible and can be fatally toxic to dogs, causing anything from diarrhea to death. Likewise, avoid things like corn on the cob. Dogs love to chew on these, but corn-cob pieces can obstruct airways and kill.

The debate about feeding is fascinating! Use any combination of plans that offer the best nutritional value. Most strongly recommended of all is the following outstanding feeding alternative.

The Bones and Appropriate Raw Food Diet

The Bones And Raw Food (or Biologically Appropriate Raw Food) diet, known by its nickname acronym "BARF," is a feeding plan that consists mostly of meaty bones and raw food. Canine nutrition specialist, Dr. Ian Billinghurst, (*The Bones and Appropriate Raw Food Diet, Give Your Dog a Bone,* and *Grow Your Pups with Bones*) explains thoroughly the benefits of feeding meaty bones and appropriate raw food to ensure better general health, stronger teeth, healthier coat, all-round better behavior, greater focus, improved attention span, and a longer life span. What could be better?

Protein, the first nutritional building block, is essential, but too much can lead to kidney failure in old age. One-third to half your pack's daily diet should consist of raw meat, easily digestible by canine stomach enzymes. Besides, they like it that way! You should include heart, kidney, gizzard, and organ meat, chicken and turkey. Give the pack raw chicken wings, necks, and backs, but not chicken or turkey legs or other bones that splinter. Never feed cooked bones because they splinter easily.

Dogs thrive on fish, too, which, besides being tasty and nutritious, improves and maintains a rich, luxurious coat and well-lubricated skin. My first puppy, Cara Mia, and I met her littermate sister when the pups were six months old. The other puppy's owner had a fish market. He boiled salmon heads every day, removed all the bones, and added the rest to her meals. Her coat was astonishingly beautiful, actually superior to Cara Mia's (which was also magnificent). Regular amounts of salmon in her diet made that pup's fur radiant and luxurious, lovely beyond description, soft, rich, and shiny.

Besides meat and fish, raw unpasteurized milk, yogurt, cottage cheese, and ricotta cheese are excellent for dogs. Even though dogs love ice cream, avoid feeding it in excess as it leads to obesity. Include regular servings of vegetables, best if raw. Give your pack fresh grated carrots, chopped broccoli, chopped green beans, crushed spinach, and Swiss chard. Juice the veggies and then mix some of the pulp back into the juice. Add it to their raw meat rations. Cooked rice, preferably brown, is excellent, as is millet, oatmeal, and other whole grains. Soak the oatmeal, and give it soaked and raw. Dogs can eat chopped nuts from time to time, and they love it. Give them apples, watermelon, grapes, bananas, cantaloupe, and strawberries. Whenever I ask my German shepherd Abby if she wants an apple, she wags her tail vigorously and heads straight for the armchair where I usually sit for my evening apple. There she happily awaits her share.

A couple of times a week, feed your dogs soft-boiled eggs, both the whites and yolks. If you feed the eggs raw, use only the yolk. My pack loves well-beaten eggs including yolk and white. Hard-boiled eggs can be given with shell and all.

Soybean oil, olive oil, flaxseed oil, and sesame oil are excellent sources of polyunsaturated fats that dogs need. Add a tablespoon to their meals several times a week, but not much more. If they have loose stools, reduce the oil. Besides being nutritional, a bit of oil adds flavor.

Even if you fully appreciate the B.A.R.F. diet, you might not be able to afford raw meat and veggies every day. You also might not have time to shop and prepare them. Nevertheless, it's a proven fact that dogs thrive on this diet. You can include it in a modified way with whatever else you decide to use.

commercial Versus Homemade Dog Food

The growing controversy about the relative benefits of commercial versus homemade dog foods has led the way to happier, healthier dogs, if not happier dog food company managers! Reflect deeply about the importance of feeding high-quality meals. As said of people, dogs, too, are what they eat. It's better to spend the money on good food than on veterinary bills. The computer adage, "Garbage in, garbage out," holds true for dog food, too.

The worst commercial dog foods include meat byproducts, that is, cow hooves, bones, skin, hair, glands, leftover organs, horns, feathers, claws, beaks, waste material, chicken and turkey feet, and other parts left behind after processing. Doesn't sound very appetizing, does it?

Dr. Will Falconer, DVM, gives us the low-down on all the ingredients we should *never* permit our dogs to eat. Dr. Falconer's 4-D category includes dead, diseased, dying, and disabled animals that arrive at the slaughterhouse unfit for consumption but find their way into commercial dog foods. This is the scandal of the lowest grade commercial dog foods. Dr. Falconer alleges that some pet food companies even use spoiled meat occasionally, and I don't doubt it. Even pets and horses that have been put to sleep are ground into the pot.

Unscrupulous manufacturers bake this disgusting mixture of slop into kibble. The mix is extruded under very high pressure and extremely hot temperatures, then coated with grease to make it palatable to the poor dogs that are fed it. The disgrace of these abominable manufacturing processes is only now coming to the fore. It is shameful. Let all serious dog lovers be alert and resist the impulse to cut corners on feeding costs by purchasing low-grade dog food. We can win the battle against these sickening commercial foods by refusing to purchase them.

Unfortunately, too many dog owners mistakenly believe meat byproducts to be acceptable ingredients in their dogs' food. This is *absolutely not so.* If you see the words "meat byproducts" on a list of ingredients, put that food back on the shelf and walk away. Buy dog foods that include only human-grade, quality ingredients. Dishonest commercial manufacturers put into their dog foods animal materials that would have to be totally rejected as food for people. The tragedy and scandal is that such foods manage to pass U.S. government inspections. False flavorings and chemical additives alter the taste and sight of seriously flawed dog food. This manipulation tricks owners into thinking that all is well. Hungry dogs don't know any better, but people should. It's not enough to see the words "veterinarian approved" or "veterinarian recommended."

Here's a quick list of ingredients to avoid in dog food:

- Animal or meat byproducts
- Soybeans
- Citrus pulps
- Corn cobs
- Fillers of any kind
- Toxic preservatives

Many diseases that beset dogs would never occur were it not for improper diets. We have the information we need to feed our dogs correctly. Avoid artificial coloring and preservatives like BHA (butylated hydroxyanisole) and BHT (butylated hydroxytoluene) that are used to add shelf life. These are toxic ingredients. So is the flavor enhancer MSG (monosodium glutamate), as well as other chemical preservatives that are implicated in the occurrence of liver and kidney disease, cancer, birth and brain defects, slow growth rates, and other deadly problems. MSG masks the taste of bad dog food while it slowly kills your canine friend.

Ethoxyquin is neither acceptable nor necessary, but it continues to be used as a preservative in many dog foods. Did you know that ethoxyquin was originally developed to preserve leather? It does *not* belong in dog food. Ethoxyquin is an herbicide—a poison, in other words. You'll find ethoxyquin listed way down in the list of ingredients named on the package, almost as if the manufacturers are trying to hide it. Never buy food products that contain ethoxyquin.

Many countries ban products that use these ingredients that are clearly unfit for canine consumption. Sadly, the United States does not. Profit is the reason. This nation's multimillion dollar pet food industry continues to take advantage of uninformed or unconcerned pet owners. Dogs can't choose the food we give them. They cannot read labels. But we can and we must. Feeding the pack properly is all about quality of life, health, and longevity.

The next level of dog foods, going upward in terms of quality, is that called premium dog food. Premium dog foods sold in pet specialty stores are usually better than supermarket brands. They provide what reasonable people ought to expect in the food they buy for their cherished canine kids. Premium dog foods cost a bit more than supermarket slop, but the money you save in veterinary care, and the grief and suffering you prevent, is worth the few extra pennies spent. When dogs are fed better brands, which are those containing human-grade meat or fish meal as the first listed ingredient, they don't need to eat as much. That's because their nutritional needs are met with less food consumption. You'll end up spending less money on food and veterinary care.

When you change over to a healthy dog food (and do it immediately if necessary) add it gradually to that which was previously used. If your pack isn't interested in making the switch at first, tempt them to the healthy choice by including some raw meat, cottage cheese, or slightly cooked eggs as you introduce the better food. Each day, slightly increase the volume of the good quality food selected and decrease that of the poorer quality. Phase one in and the other out and never look back.

These are among the most excellent, high-quality dog foods available:

- Best Breed Dog Food
- California Natural
- Innova
- Wellness
- Wysong
- Nutro All Natural
- Flint River Ranch Dog Food
- Canidae
- AvoDerm Health Food for Dogs by Breeders Choice
- Sojourner Farms European Style Pet Food

Food Guarding

Most dogs are instinctively wired to guard their food. From an early age, give and take your pack's food away at will, not to tease or torment, but to assert your alpha position and avoid future troubles connected with food guarding. Alpha eats first in the wild. Be sure you eat first, too.

Every dog needs to have its own dish or bowl. Serve the pack individually and separately one from another. Crates make terrific individual doggie restaurants where food guarding is avoided simply because it's not necessary. Dogs instinctively know that they are king in their own crates. Their food bowls, placed inside their crates, are safe from attack by doggie hogs in the pack. Feeding in their crates eliminates food stealing. Your dogs will be more calm as they eat, assured that food guarding tactics are not needed to fend off scavengers looking for more. This prevents fights and ensures that feeding time is under control.

Keep a feeding schedule at the same time twice daily, but don't worry if you're sometimes a little late or a little early. Although they thrive on routine, dogs readily adjust to changes if they're not too drastic. If you walk your pack separately and want to feed them after walking, you can still feed the group at the same time by letting the first walkers wait. Keep fresh water available in a common area accessible to the pack. Dogs don't fight over the water bowl. If your dogs are the exception and like a little action when drinking, put down another bowl someplace else.

Chapter 8

Dog Time and People Time

A dog is the only thing on earth
that loves you more than he loves himself.
—Josh Billings

A colleague of mine once said, "In the final analysis the only currency we have is time itself, and once we spend it, it's gone forever." Our dogs are with us for a relatively short period of time, considering the length of the average human lifespan and theirs. If we're lucky, some hardy canines might live ten, twelve, or even fourteen years, but longevity is a gift, not a promise, and dog lives are short by human standards.

Make the best of those hours you spend with the pack, whether in training, grooming, feeding, playing, or just hanging out. In living with dogs, time is truly the main currency, but money and energy are a big part of the investment, too. The return is unlimited. Dogs give back to us in such abundance, offering the totality of their companionship, loyalty, and protection, returning unconditional love for the currency of our time.

If you want to keep a multi-dog household, be ready to commit a certain portion of every day to meeting canine needs. For the last twenty-five years, I have spent enormous blocks of time with dogs, hours upon hours with my own and others, sharing information and enthusiasm for pack life with dog owners everywhere. I do not regret any of it. Dogs have gifted my life with riches beyond words.

Dog Time

In your multi-dog home, dog time is particularly important. Dogs measure time by a mysterious inner clock and calendar that coincides with ours but has its own variables. Sharing the world of their human counterparts, dogs seem to know exactly when it's time to eat, sleep, or play. They tell us, too, in their own language of a nudge, whine, bark, or paw on one's thigh. Take me out. Fill my bowl. Throw this ball. Dogs keep us from getting lost in human time and forgetting their needs. They read the hours intuitively, knowing exactly when we should return from work each day. They lie beside us in the darkness, companions of the night, eager to greet us at the coming of dawn. They know the schedule of our days and travel through our calendar years, marking their way with loyalty and love.

Dogs are regular about everything. Their internal clocks mark the natural flow of all the seasons throughout their lives from puppy to old age. Becoming attuned to the way dogs measure time is not a matter of philosophical speculation or scientific explanation. It's just a connection with nature at an elemental level. Pack life has a rhythm that meshes with ours. Dogs wait patiently for the folks they love, eager to share the gift of time.

I've always found the pack to be programmed for a perfect fit into the human scheme of things. Dogs accommodate our human schedules with amazing ease. The time patterns we create become habits for the pack that ensure their comfort and our peace of mind. Although they know intuitively when it's time to eat, sleep, play, or do business outdoors, our dogs wait patiently for us to make it happen.

How Much Time Should You Spend with Your Dogs?

The time you spend with your dogs must first of all be *quality* time. Many years ago, when I was a nun in the monastery at New Skete, I met Ms. Helen "Scootie" Sherlock, nationally known breeder of German shepherd dogs and AKC trial judge. Scootie often visited the monastery as friend to the monks and nuns and advisor in their German shepherd breeding program. Scootie's influence helped shape the destiny of New Skete German shepherds, and in a way, mine, too.

On one occasion, as a novice dog handler working with my first monastery dog, Natasha, I asked Ms. Sherlock just how much time dogs need from a person's busy life. Scootie said that dogs need at least an hour a day of quality time. That has been my rule of thumb for the last three decades. It doesn't mean you have to spend an hour a day with each dog individually, or that it must be *exactly* one hour per day. You can take the pack out walking together or stay at home with them and just sit around. The quality time dogs need is companionship with their people. This is *not* feeding time, *not* grooming time, and *not* sleeping time, but time in which dog and people interact together, attentive to one another, interlocking their energies and sharing in play, work, or rest. In a very real sense, there's a contemplative and mystical element here in the time we spend deeply connected with our animals, a spiritual experience as well as a physical one.

What Dogs Need Most from Their People

My dogs (probably yours, too) wait patiently for hours, lying at my feet while I am busy at the computer or talking on the phone. In fact, dogs are *always* waiting for something. Maybe that's what "It's a dog's life" means.

Dogs wait for us to meet their basic needs and share their canine lives. They wait for our attention, the *only* attention they crave. They wait for us to fulfill their minimal rights to food, drink, walks, play, and other social interactions. They wait for us to become attuned to their animal presence and penetrate the mist that separates one species from another. Communication is the heart of time-sharing with the pack.

Unless you're willing to invest a good portion of your precious time to meet the needs of the pack, don't keep dogs. Don't even have *one* dog. People with no time to spare cannot do justice to animals and shouldn't have any. It's quite unfair to forget about your dogs once accustomed to the pack and neglect them in favor of other pursuits you prefer over dog duties. Dogs need you from the moment they enter your life to the moment they depart. Time issues are a critical consideration in living with the pack. The choice is always yours, the human's, *not* the dogs', but once you choose to make this commitment, be true to them as they are true to you.

I recall the unforgettable legend of a great Akita dog that continued to stand and wait at a subway entrance in a Japanese city, looking for its person to return home after work. The dog stayed on long after the man had died and no longer came and went that way. This exemplifies the way dogs handle time.

My dogs love to sit or lie near the kitchen door and watch me while I prepare their meals or mine. They hover near the bathroom or bedroom, wherever I am. They greet me when I come and go, ever vigilant, ever hopeful, delighting in each moment spent together. Dogs are an integral part of family life, never tiring of their people, bonded forever.

When Packs Don't Get What They Need from People

Deprived of human attention, dogs become uncomfortable and unhappy. They often search for release from these unpleasant emotions. Individually or in the pack, dogs get into trouble when they're bored, lonely, hungry, or restless—in other words, when they don't get the time they need from their people. Here are a few of the ways dogs can choose to occupy themselves.

- **"I think I'll just explore a bit."** Dogs nose their way into places and things you never wanted them to get into.
- **"I think I'll sniff this item that smells so much like Mom or Pop, and maybe nibble it just a bit."** Dogs chew whatever attracts their fancy, particularly items that bear your scent, such as your furniture, clothing, slippers, shoes and socks, or even the tiles on the kitchen floor.
- **"I think I'll check this out for food."** Bored and neglected dogs raid the garbage can or climb aboard kitchen counters to harvest anything edible.
- **"Maybe I should mark my territory."** Dogs pee here and there when stressed, squirting the couch or furniture leg, marking near the door, delineating their world, more likely than not, because of longing for you.
- **"I should call Mom and Pop."** One dog starts to whine and bark and soon, its packmates join in. Now we have a living, breathing, barking serenade of loneliness, neglect, boredom, and hunger. The neighbors don't like it.

This behavior is never the dogs' fault. It's ours. Dogs are not capable of vindictiveness or spite; those emotions require a kind of thinking that is simply incompatible with their nature.

They don't chew, dig, scratch, urinate, defecate, or bark incessantly out of a desire to get even. They act and react from loneliness, boredom, separation anxiety, hunger, and restlessness. Their unmet legitimate needs fuel destructive behaviors in dogs the same as they do in human children.

I have worked in the New York City Department of Probation for the past fifteen years, where I've seen hundreds of youngsters pass through the family court system. These kids are in trouble because of neglect, boredom, loneliness, hunger, and restlessness. In other words, the important people in their lives just "didn't have time" for them. They commit real crimes, sometimes heinous ones.

Dogs can only commit doggie crimes, but their misadventures often appear just as criminal to angry owners coming home tired at night to find the house in chaos. It's sad to say but true that many of the kids in family court cannot be rescued. Things have already gone too far in their young lives. They often revert back to gang life and street crimes. The few we can save are the lucky ones. Kids and dogs have this important principle in common: left to themselves, they struggle for release from restless energy and depression. When kids or dogs don't get the time they need to spend with their important people, a terrible void opens up in their hearts and souls. Their worlds collapse, and chaos follows.

People often get rid of troublesome dogs without realizing that they, themselves, created the problem. By examining the reasons behind doggie mischief, disgruntled owners could change the destiny of these hapless canines that find themselves dumped at the pound or shelter, often put to sleep for no fault of their own. Their people just didn't have time for them.

The way to achieve harmony in your multi-dog home, or even with a single pet, is to put the necessary time into it and make each moment work. Health and happiness, theirs and yours, result from investing quality time with the pack. We must commit ourselves to the absolute eradication of neglect—in all its forms.

How to Manage Several Dogs and Still Have a Life of Your Own

Now you might be wondering if there's ever going to be time left for you in your multi-dog home. As a pack parent, can you have a life of your own? Of course you can. In order to enjoy time for yourself, take care of the pack first. After the dogs are taken care of, fed, exercised, and all the rest, you can enjoy the peace and tranquility of a well-run household. Dogs cannot understand reasons for lengthy delays in the fulfillment of their needs, so if you first attend to them, you'll have a quiet satisfied pack that allows you to do for yourself whatever makes you happy.

You don't have to banish your dogs from family activities if they are properly trained. On occasions when you feel they must be kept out of sight, give them plenty of exercise first and sufficient food and water before retiring them to crate, yard, or kennel. Wherever you leave them on their own, provide them with diversionary toys, playthings to entertain themselves. Keep such toys away from the pack until you need to leave your dogs while you're busy elsewhere.

Well-behaved dogs can be a part of nondoggie activities in ways you might never imagine. I used to take my East German shepherd dog, Grip, to a little Russian Orthodox church where I regularly attended Saturday night vespers. It was a long drive from home, and I enjoyed Grip's company on the way. During the service, Grip remained quietly in the back of the church, lying down with his huge body half in the priest's office and half in the nave of the church. From this vantage point, Grip could see me standing in the choir near the icon screen by the altar. One time, the altar boy didn't show up to serve with the priest. At the point in the service where the priest came down from the altar, swinging the incense and chanting prayers as he stood before an icon stand in the center of the nave, Grip quietly left his spot in back of the church and walked to the middle of the nave to stand reverently beside the priest. The great dog seemed to intend taking the place of the absent altar boy who usually stood in this spot. Needless to say, "Brother Grip" was quickly removed from the scene, but not without endearing himself to priest and congregation alike. Many churches hold special services to bless the beasts every year on the feast of St. Francis of Assisi. They warmly welcome furry families in attendance with their pack parents.

It takes more time to deal with the needs of several dogs than only one, and larger dogs, I believe, require even more time. The following guidelines will help you establish a good routine for managing your multi-dog home and still have a life of your own:

- Maintain a regular routine.
- Take the dogs out for duty and exercise several times a day.
- Feed the dogs on schedule twice daily and provide fresh water.
- Give them stay-at-home pack toys, bones, or other amusement to help entertain them during your absence.
- Go off and enjoy a life of your own, doing what you want, but don't expect that a morning walk will suffice for a twelve-hour absence or longer. That would be unfair.

Dog Depression and owner Guilt

We all know the pang of leaving dogs behind. They watch us dress and prepare to go out, looking hopefully toward their leashes and collars, waiting while we get ready and then following us to the door in hopes of accompanying us on our way. Going to work and other places where dogs can't come demands periods of separation that fill some dogs with depression and not a few owners with guilt.

Dogs are creatures of habit. They soon acquire new habits when given half a chance, so be patient in teaching your pack that when you leave, you *will* return. For each new member in the pack, go through the basic separation steps to acclimate the newcomer and reinforce training with the oldsters about alpha's departure and return. Here's how:

- Get ready to leave the house.
- Say a short, nonemotional goodbye.
- Close the door and return in a little while.
- Increase the length of your absence gradually.

Soon your dogs will understand that alpha comes and goes at will, but always returns. Never leave young dogs or small ones, puppy or adult, alone with larger mature animals. Unfortunate accidents can happen because unpredictable behavior erupts unexpectedly even in the best-trained pack. Separate the smaller, weaker dogs from the larger, stronger ones when you're absent.

Be sure your pack never has free access to small children, infants, toddlers, or youngsters of grammar school age. Never leave dogs tied up outside, where they can become problems for neighbors or aggressive toward strangers trying to approach. By following these basic considerations of canine safety, you will secure your pack during every absence.

Enough diversionary toys are necessary to eliminate competition among the pack members while you go about your business without guilt.

A better idea is to crate each dog separately while you're out. You must be the judge of whether or not to crate. For most dogs, a raw meaty bone makes an excellent babysitter. Raw meaty bones are fantastic pacifiers and very nourishing besides. Although some trainers recommend offering dogs pig ears, cow hooves, rawhide, and other chewies in your absence, I worry about dogs choking on softened articles of this kind. Leaving dogs behind with diversionary toys and treats often eliminates or at least reduces canine depression when owners are absent. (Human depression about leaving the pack must be resolved by using reason and intelligence. Dogs don't need therapy for this, but sometimes owners do!)

Dogs get bored with the same old thing. Rotate the toys you leave for them when you're out of the house so that each new occasion provides something interesting to hold their attention. This doesn't need to become a financial strain. Recycle toys by removing them for a few days, and the pack will take notice when they reappear. Provide several toys per dog to eliminate the possibility of guarding or stealing confrontations.

Dogs adjust to our schedules. They lie down and fall asleep much more easily than their worried humans can. They don't toss and turn because you're out of the house; they are not alarmed when you stay out past curfew. They need to relieve themselves, so make some provision for elimination, even a newspaper spread in some hidden corner. Don't get ruffled when you find a puddle or poop to clean up after a longer absence than usual. Once you depart, dogs usually drift off to sleep. Their time passes quite effortlessly, so don't feed your guilt by imagining your mutts pacing the floor worrying about you, wondering if traffic is holding you up or something is wrong with the car. Although no one in all the world will be quite as happy as your mutts to welcome you home, like it or not, they must accept the fact that alpha comes and goes at will. As they mature, your pack will take your absences more and more in stride.

Avoid overly demonstrative greetings or goodbyes. Make your comings and goings casual by keeping your tone of voice very matter-of-fact. Believe it or not, this eases separation anxiety.

Chapter 9

Games Dogs Play (with Their People)

I loathe people who keep dogs. They are cowards who haven't got the guts to bite people themselves.
—August Strindberg

D ogs love to play, and they readily learn new games. They thrive mentally and physically on regular play and burn off energy that might otherwise lead to destructive behavior. Playing with the pack is one of life's most pleasurable activities, but to enjoy it to the hilt, you have to let go and be a dog for awhile. Don't worry about getting hair on your clothes. Drop your burdens and your cares. Don't be distracted by the pressures of life. Just get in there and play. You'll be young again, carefree and happy. The pack will show you how!

I had a German shepherd named Geisty who actually created games. Every morning of her life, from the time she arrived until the day she died, Geisty came to my pillow at break of day and placed a toy near my face. Then she went off and got another. Determined to get it right and rouse me into action, Geisty brought her horde of playthings to my bed every single morning at first light of dawn. When she had puppies of her own, she created games for them and taught them how to play. It was obvious that Geisty was meant to be our pack's social director.

Having fun with the pack makes all the work worthwhile. Dogs are wildly enthusiastic about having fun. For them, it seems, the fun increases exponentially with the number of participants. Maybe the first human-and-dog teams that emerged eons ago happened when cavemen noticed pack play among the first domesticated canines and thought they'd like to get involved.

Games for Dogs and People

Some cities provide parks and fields where dogs can run free with their humans enjoying outdoor fun. Wherever you live, investigate your options, and be creative with whatever space is available. The best games are those that require vigorous activity. Having fun is safest in places far from traffic. You can modify dog activities to fit into the available space. Go for it.

Benefits of Play

Playing games with the pack includes these benefits for dogs and people:

- Physical exercise prevents obesity.
- Games help develop coordination, muscular endurance, and physical strength.
- Playing is mentally stimulating and exhilarating.
- Physical activities provide emotional release and improve bonding between dogs and people.
- Playing with the pack ensures better discipline.
- Problem-solving in games helps dogs learn to figure things out.
- Playtime increases the development of socialization skills.
- Vigorous games lead to appetite improvement and muscle development.
- Pack play sustains a sense of shared purpose and cohesiveness in the multi-dog home.

When neighbors see me playing with my dogs, they refer to it as the Brooklyn version of "dancing with wolves." Playing with the pack engenders such a sense of well-being that there's no need for intellectual justification. I know some dog parents who live by the clock of dog fun with their daily trips to the park and beach or whatever venue is best for them.

In this chapter, I will discuss some activities that I've enjoyed with my pack over the years. I'll also include dog games written about by the experts. Fun and exercise are at the core of a healthy lifestyle for you and your pack. I hope this chapter helps you improve the quality of game time with your dogs.

Tug o' War

As with most pack games, you can make up the rules for tug o' war as you go along. You can change them later or stick to them at will. This is a dog game perfectly tailored for the pack. Canines love to bite hard into an object that is attached to a human at the other end or even one held in the bite of other dogs. The incredible strength of a dog's bite is demonstrated over and over again in the game of tug o' war. Rolled up old towels make great tugging things. Nowadays, you can purchase sophisticated, rope-like tugs, soft rubber squeaky tugs, or burlap or canvas rolled tugs. All of these are made with or without handles.

Dogs love pulling on tugs and getting them out of your grasp. Puppies and dogs need to achieve success in the game of tug o' war, so let them win most of the time. As you release the tug, praise your dog. It's harder to play with two or three tugging beasts, but it's great fun for the pack and a hefty challenge for you.

Start puppies off in tug o' war separate from the pack, so

the pup has a chance to win. Winning builds self-confidence. Later on, let the puppy join in the pack tug. Use the game to teach young dogs how to grab and hold an object. Praise them, saying "Take it" or "Hold it." Then, gently offer resistance. Allow the pup to win by letting go of your end and praising. Say something like, "Good dog. You got it!" Eventually, you can teach the release command, "Drop it" or "Give" or "Out" by taking hold of the tug and gently blowing into the nostrils of your dog until it opens its mouth and lets go. Whichever word you choose to command, stick with it. Dogs learn by associating an action with a word.

Tug o' war is a great game for building obedience into fun activities. When dogs are most attentive, take the object and give them the down-stay command. Move forward some distance and put the tug down on the ground. Now the dogs must wait until you return to them and send them off saying, "Go, find." When the first dog there picks up the tug, let it carry it around triumphantly while you praise the whole pack.

Fetch

Fetch is doggie heaven brought to Earth! Dogs love chasing whatever object, ball, tug, or stick you toss into the distance, releasing them full force to get it. There are even mechanical launches to shoot fetch objects into the air. If you have enough tennis balls and a good arm, hit them out with a tennis racquet until every dog in your pack is running headlong into the field flying in pursuit. From puppy days, you should teach dogs to return their fetch objects for another shot. Visit tennis courts in your area and ask for dead tennis balls. They are glad to turn them over to you, and your pack won't care how dead they are. They make great toys for dogs.

I have always played these games with several dogs at the same time. Somehow or other, dogs seem to understand words like, "It's Geisty's turn. Wait." Just don't keep other pack members waiting too long for their turns. If your dog doesn't return the item, remedy the situation by attaching its collar to a long line and reeling it in carefully while saying, "Bring" or "Fetch." A forty-foot-long, one-inch-wide lead works fine. Keep the line out of the way as you let the dog run out fully to get its booty. When you reel it in, bring the dog to a front sit and praise it, gently stroking the forehead while the dog retains the fetched object. Then, calmly give the command "Drop it" or "Give." If the dog hesitates releasing the object, gently blow into its nostrils. You can also grasp the animal's mouth and apply some pressure to the area around its canine teeth, where slight discomfort will encourage Fido to give it up. Dogs will play fetch until your arm falls off. They don't get tired; we do. Any article you can get airborne makes a great fetch toy. The same goodies can be used for the following search game.

Go Find

Hide-and-seek is a variation of good old fetch. You can teach hide-and-seek outdoors or in the relative comfort of home. First, be sure your dogs can execute a reasonably sound down-stay. Take the object(s) of interest, and let the dogs see that you have it as you walk a short distance away and put it down within their sight. Don't release them to go find until you have returned to their sides. The first one to arrive at the article wins, but everybody gets a treat when they return to you.

Go Find lends itself to many variations. Eventually, you can make it a preliminary exercise in search and rescue training. Dogs can smell things hidden underwater, underground, and up

in the air. My pack has easily located objects hidden underwater, underground, or in a tree or bush limb. Let a friend or
family member walk away from the dogs, into the wind, while
you hold the pack. Have the person hide. After an agreed upon
number of minutes, release the pack with the command "Go
find!" The first dog that reaches the hidden person is the
acclaimed victor, but the whole pack shares in the hunt, and
everybody gets a treat for reward.

Frisbee

Never much of a Frisbee fan myself, I am nonetheless
enchanted by the sight of small dogs leaping up into the air to
catch the soaring disc. Pet stores supply Frisbees of every kind
and color, cloth ones being better than hard rubber or plastic.
A soft Frisbee is just as much fun to throw and chase after, and
your dogs won't break a tooth catching it. Frisbee competitions
have become all the rage in some places. Several Frisbees can
be launched in relatively quick succession for everybody in the
pack to play.

There's really not a lot of difference playing most games
with several dogs or playing them with just one. You get better
at it with practice. Your own creativity and enthusiasm are the
only limit in playing with dogs.

The Nose Knows

An indoor game I loved to play with my first monastery dog
years ago lends itself more to a house setting. But it works
about as well in an apartment, except that there's less terrain
to cover. Several dogs can play at the same time (that is, if you
can tolerate the noise and excitement generated by the hunt).

There are plenty of places to hide things in the house, and there is less likelihood that the neighbors will get annoyed with the noise than if you play this game in an apartment setting.

Acquaint the pack with the object of the search, letting them sniff and bite it, hold it, and so on. Put the dogs in a down-stay. Go off to another room, and hide the thing. Then return and send them to find it. Let the dogs see what you're doing at first, even hiding it in the same room so they'll get the idea. It's amazing how well their noses work to sniff out the object even though your scent and its are everywhere in the house. Still, they search and find it.

Gradually increase the level of difficulty, and hide the object in another room, hallway, or closet. Place the object partially out of sight at first, then hide it completely. When you return to the room where the dogs are waiting, quietly go to them and say, "Go find." The dogs do get a little rambunctious as they run off in search of the object, and quite excited when they return with one dog waving the prize in its grin. Let the dog enjoy its booty for a little bit, and then give the command: "Out" or "Drop it." Gently blow into its nostrils if it refuses to give it up immediately.

Sometimes, it's fun to hide yourself instead of an object. Put your dogs in a down-stay and leave the room. Hide anywhere in the house, in a closet, under a bed, behind a door, beside a chair, under a table, wherever you can fit. When you're ready, call to them, "Go find," and enjoy watching them track you down.

Finally, leave a trail of food treats indoors while the dogs are waiting in their crates or in a long down-stay. Place small pieces of delicious-smelling treats, like hot dogs or turkey, in various hiding spots. Put the treats partially or entirely out of sight, and be sure they are sufficient in quantity to make it worth their while. The more they love the bait, the better their "Go find" will be. Whoever has the best nose and moves the fastest will find and gobble the most treats. Be sure to give a little help to the youngest or least capable, just to keep everyone happy. By the way, planting treats in various places around the apartment or home for a single dog to find when you go out is excellent diversionary fun. Don't try this with a pack, however, since in your absence they might fight over every find.

There are no set rules about doggie games unless you plan to enter competitions. Make whatever adjustments you need to ensure that your pack gets totally involved. Don't stifle them with a fastidious need of your own for orderliness or quiet. The object of games is fun. Keep on experimenting with variations on all these games.

Tracking

Tracking is a more sophisticated dog sport. Tracking is the canine art of finding an object or person by following a scent trail, either with a deep nose, head to the ground, scenting footsteps along the way, or air scenting and sniffing bushes and other vegetation where the person has fled. There are several versions of tracking as a competitive sport, and each has its own special rules. You can find groups in the area near your home that are dedicated to Schutzhund tracking or AKC tracking, each slightly different from the other. If you plan to compete, you must learn the rules carefully and apply them in many practice sessions as you prepare your dog for engagement. Otherwise, there are lots of creative variations you might introduce to the game of tracking. It's a great pleasure to watch dogs following a scent trail, their noses twitching with enthusiasm as they lock on the scent.

Scent lingers wherever we pass, and dogs are greatly attuned to these avenues of smell. Professional tracking dogs can travel enormous distances in advance of a search party, never losing the scent they are trailing after. They even recognize the air scent that might blow back to them from an open window of the escaping vehicle. Professional tracking dogs can determine immediately whether the search object has stopped at a roadside gas station or restaurant.

Tracking is easy to teach because it's really what comes naturally to dogs. Put the dog in a place apart, such as the car or in its crate, a few yards away from the beginning point of your track. Stomp out a small four-foot square and place a few good smelly treats (tiny cuts of hot dog or turkey) on every other footprint. After the scent box is laid, make a small trail, keeping some object like a tree in sight so you'll walk straight to the end of the track. Put a treat in the heel of each footprint. Some folks put little flag markers in the ground to help them remember their route and to know if the dogs are going correctly once they begin to follow the track. Walk the distance you determine, which shouldn't be too long at first, and take long, graceful strides. Wait about fifteen minutes for the track to "age" or "season." That means the scent starts to rise from your footprints, creating a kind of smelly corridor that the dogs will follow. Take your dogs, one at a time, to the starting point, the four-foot square scent box you laid at the beginning. Point to the first step and give the command, "Find it." Dogs pick up the object scent right away because that's just their nature. Given a chance, this natural ability comes to the fore. If you plan to compete, get the rules for the particular competition and follow them. Otherwise, just be creative and enjoy!

Herding

I've read a lot about herding and sheep tending, but I've never actually participated in these activities with my dogs, so what I can offer you here is quite rudimentary. If it stirs your interest, there are many sources for further learning about herding.

Dogs with the right kind of prey drive are natural herders and sheep tenders. Of course, you need to get access to a field and some sheep if you want to try it out. A nonherding dog would probably just as soon munch on the sheep as guide them into an appropriate place, such as a designated enclosure.

To participate in herding, dogs must be reliable in basic obedience even if commanded from a distance. They must be able to concentrate on the sheep, to stop and stay on command, to go back into action when released from the stop and stay command, and to come when called. The natural ability to herd is readily seen in such breeds as German shepherds, Shetland sheepdogs, Australian shepherds, Border collies, and other herding breeds.

If you want to get into herding with your dogs, check out the resource section in the appendix of this book. You can also visit Web sites devoted to this activity. Best of all, try to find a sheep herding group near you and give it a try. You'll be glad you did, and so will your dog!

Agility

Agility is fun for an individual dog and great for the pack. It requires that dogs and handlers move quickly with skill through a number of obstacles. Dogs become highly focused and excited when running the agility course. For competitions, naturally, you must learn and observe the rules properly, but for personal family fun, just enjoy running the course, managing the obstacles along the way. Agility keeps dogs (and their handlers) in shape and sharpens awareness. Maneuvering through the obstacles is a real challenge, increasing with difficulty as dogs and people become more skillful at the sport. There are hurdles, tunnels, poles, and other obstacles to navigate. You can do agility with your whole pack as long as you're not in a real competition, which is an activity for handler and a single dog. Dogs are naturally agile. Their innate curiosity sparks them into exploring nooks and crannies that require a certain amount of dexterity and balance to reach and return from safely.

The first agility demonstration took place in England in 1979 at the Crufts Dog Show. Since then, the sport of dog agility has mushroomed everywhere. Equipment for agility training is easily obtained. You can make it yourself out of PVC piping, readily available in most hardware stores. Simply build the different structures for the course and fashion them in such a way that dogs will not injure themselves if they misjudge distances or heights.

The obstacles used in most agility playgrounds vary in size and types, including different sorts of jumps, hoops and tunnels, an A-frame which the dog will climb and descend, poles placed at intervals for weaving in and out, and other hindrances to free running. You start slowly and eventually progress through the obstacle course at top speed. The idea is for the dogs to get through the course quickly and efficiently. You run it, too, directing the dog at its work, moving alongside the hurdles, climbs, etc. You may not touch the dog or the equipment, but only give verbal support. To learn the "real deal" about agility, contact the North American Dog Agility Council, Inc. (NADAC) at 11522 South Hwy 3, Cataldo, ID, 83810. Or check out their Web site at *www.nadac.com.*

Sledding

Sledding is essentially a team sport, so what could be better for the multi-dog home than getting engaged in sledding? The sport depends on the coordinated efforts of a dog team, running together in harness dragging a load. Even if you have no dreams of running the Iditarod and no ancestral connection with the ancient Eskimo of northern Alaska who produced marvelous sled dogs, like the Alaskan malamutes—or the Chuckchi people of northeastern Siberia who created Siberian huskies—you might be drawn to the fun of dog sledding just the same.

A fatal diphtheria epidemic in 1925 threatened to wipe out the population of Nome, Alaska. Dogs came to the fore, making it through where planes could not go because of the extreme cold. Serum had to be brought from Anchorage, Alaska, to Nenana and on to Nome. Many lives were at stake. The risks were incredible, but the dogs and their handlers proved themselves heroic. The serum they carried traveled by dog sled 674 miles across the barren, frozen, terrain, making the journey in less than a week! This historic journey resulted in saving many lives and is commemorated annually in the great Iditarod sled dog race of Alaska. The Internet today allows the journey of Iditarod runners to be tracked online for those of us who must remain armchair mushers. Even if you don't have dogs that are bred for sledding, you can do your amateur sledding events for fun and get your pack involved in pulling something by their joint effort.

Mushing means driving sled dogs. It's not a command but an activity. Once in harness, sled dogs respond to the language of mushers, but we don't need to go into that vocabulary in a book like this. Mushing equipment includes the sled, harness, ganglines, sled bags, snow hooks, and booties for the pack. Before you attempt it, do some research to learn more about mushing, how to do it correctly, and how to enjoy this highly athletic activity. You can get started by reading Bella Levorsen's book, *Mush! A Beginner's Manual of Sled Dog Training,* or *The Joy of Running Sled Dogs* by Noel K. Flanders. Even if you don't intend to venture into the frozen north or harness your pack to a sled right here in the good old continental U.S.A., you'll probably enjoy being an armchair musher when you dig into these books. But if you want to try it out on your own, carefully follow the basic instructions. Don't so much aim at speed or endurance to begin with, but rather, just get yourself and the dogs accustomed to working as a team to pull the sled or toboggan.

Dancing with Dogs

Put on the music and spin around with your pack. That's the essence of dancing with dogs. Group dancing with dogs and people is creative moves to music; it's entertaining, and it's terrific fun. By implementing appropriate heeling steps, turns, and recalls, you can dance with your dogs to any rhythm you enjoy. Canine partners can follow quite well, adapting to our heeling techniques and musical movements. Believe it or not, some folks have actually raised this fun to the fine art of competitive freestyle routines. There are shows and competitions in many countries where judges rate the creative and competitive ability of the dog-and-person dance team!

Dancing with dogs is so much fun that even if you never read a book on it, or see a Web site about the sport, you'll have a great time designing your own dances. You might even introduce dog dancing into your own circle of dogs and people. That's how it all got started anyway. For competitions involving only one dog and one person, judges look at the quality of artistic expression, musical interpretation, and difficulty and precision of movements. Most of all, they judge on the basis of the dog's level of interest and enthusiasm. This idea has really caught on in Canada where Val Culpin, created musical freestyle as a new dog show activity. E-mail her at *Val_Culpin@ bc.sympatico.ca* if you have questions or want to learn more. Val Culpin has written online that she would love to give further information to interested parties.

Running with the Pack

Running with the pack is one of my favorite dog activities. It seems linked to the fundamental call of the wild. Wolves, coyotes, foxes, and all manner of four-legged carnivores streak across the panorama of wilderness in which they make their homes, running, running, running, crossing boundaries of time and terrain. City-bound mortals that we are, we can share in the mystical rhythm of paws during a morning jog or evening run with the pack. Running keeps you attuned to your own body and the dogs you love. It is healthful and healing. For more than a quarter century, running with dogs has served me well; in it, I have found multiple spiritual and psychological blessings.

The concept of roadwork with dogs was not new to me when I came to Brooklyn and started my own pack. At the monastery of New Skete, I was instructed by the monks to run my German shepherd as a way of getting her back in shape after weaning her pups. From the first, I loved to bicycle or run my pack along the beach at Rockaway or on the old abandoned airstrips at Floyd Bennett Field. It was not only a time of mutual exercise and physical restoration but a moving temple of meditation, feet pounding the pavement giving time to think and pray. Greeting the dawn with this pack activity, above all others, has been the mainstay of my life in New York City, energizing me to meet the challenges of keeping dogs in an urban landscape.

Several times a week, I loaded up bicycle and gear and drove out to Floyd Bennett Field or Old Fort Tilden in search of whatever peaceful remnants of wilderness I could find, just a stone's throw from the busy fourth-largest city in the country, Brooklyn, New York. In that place we walked, ran, and soared as the mood grabbed us, pack and pack mom, stillness and motion fused together and difficult to comprehend, something you must feel to understand. Running my pack nurtured my soul.

When we returned home, our neighborhood was still asleep deep in the embrace of the night. No one was about, and all was silent and still. These runs gave my pack total contentment and made them so easy to manage, all their exuberance and high energy spent on the road near the shore. No matter where you live, check out places available for you to run your dogs off lead. You can jog, rollerblade, or bicycle without worrying about traffic or other dogs and people. Your pack will soar as will your spirit.

Pointers for Running Dogs

If you want to run dogs, pay attention to these pointers:

- Respect the size, body build, and strength of the dog runner.
- Don't try to run with dogs that cannot tolerate intense workouts, such as extremely large dogs, very furry ones, dogs prone to hip dysplasia or other physical defects, or

dogs unable to keep up with you on account of size, age, or other physical conditions.

- Check their paws frequently. Running on pavement is a killer, so use dirt-packed surfaces or grass rather than the roadway and avoid concrete and hot asphalt.
- Take time off; don't run every single day. Dog muscles and yours need rest.
- Build up to your running program slowly by consistently increasing distance and endurance.
- Be careful of vehicular traffic. If you must use a thoroughfare, be sure you face oncoming traffic and keep your dogs on leash.
- Help your pack stay focused by snapping the lead abruptly to bring them back to attention and awareness of their surroundings; distractions can be dangerous.
- Run for fun, not competition, and give yourself plenty of time to learn how. Avoid crowds and other dogs, particularly dogs that are off lead and strays.

There you have it! Listen to your own call of the wild.

Roughhousing with Dogs

Some of us are real roughnecks and love to get our dogs all revved up in play. Dog dancing and dog wrestling are two fun activities that let you get involved very vigorously with the pack. You can start out with one dog alone, and gradually, as you and your canine partner learn to dance or wrestle effectively and safely, add other members of the pack until you're all roughhousing together. If you've got hundred-pounders in your pack, maybe you should keep these activities small and harmless, probably one dog at a time.

This is totally creative play that is meant to achieve one goal: vigorous interaction between you and your dogs. Dogs can unintentionally hurt you. I've had my fair share of bruises and even a few bites, but they resulted from my playing too rough and my dogs getting lost in the good time we were having. It's up to you to set limits. Play rough if you want to, but do it at your own risk and understand the consequences of wrestling with dogs.

Don't permit your dogs to jump up on anyone but yourself and even then only on command and only when you're rough-housing. Revving them up clues dogs that it's okay to put their paws on your shoulders or chest. They should not be allowed to jump on you in other situations. If at first they do not seem able to differentiate, training will help you clarify for them the situations in which they can get very rough and when they can't. When dogs jump up in play, encourage them and praise them. But when they jump up at times that they shouldn't, give the jumper your knee in the chest and say in a serious voice: "Off!"

You have to take full responsibility for your dogs' behavior. If you let them play rough, understand that control is essential. When play is through, the dogs return to a gentle, obedient behavior. My big, boisterous German shepherds love to play rough—with me—but they never show any inclination to rough up other people. When I'm engaged with my pack on the street, kids join us enthusiastically, and there's a perfect opportunity to teach kids about dogs and explain to them the responsibilities attached to rough and tumble play.

Pulling and Carting

Dogs love pulling things. Check with your vet if you want to engage in harness work like pulling and carting with your pack.

Avoid overexertive exercise in too-warm weather, and wet down your dogs if you work them on a hot day. Dogs don't sweat. Their panting indicates how hot they are. Take precautions against overheating. Whenever possible, let them run and pull on grass rather than pavement—paw pads can be easily damaged by too much activity on rough surfaces. Some dogs compete in pulling and the object is to see which dogs can pull the heaviest loads. Never push your dog to work beyond its ability. Carefully find out about any sport you intend to enjoy with your pack.

The best thing about trying all these new activities with your pack is the mutual stimulation of engaging in something different. It triggers a shared sense of adventure. Keep in mind that this is all about having fun with dogs. They'll pick up on your mood every time, so if you get out there to have fun, so will they. If you're happy, they're happy. That's just the way it is.

Chapter 10

Going Away: Travels with and Without the Pack

He is your friend, your partner, your defender, your dog. You are his life, his love, his leader. He will be yours, faithful and true, to the last beat of his heart. You owe it to him to be worthy of such devotion.

—Anonymous

When I was a novice nun at the monastery of New Skete, Brother Peter gave me a sound piece of advice as he handed me my first German shepherd puppy. "Remember, Sister Theresa," he said, "*you* are this puppy's whole world. You have another world, your life, your friends, your family, but *you* are the whole universe for this puppy. All her happiness and well-being depends on you." I never forgot Brother Peter's words of wisdom. He was so right!

We are the whole world for our dogs. Even those in packs form individual attachments to their alpha person. When alpha is absent, the entire pack misses its human, and its world is somewhat lopsided. Sometimes, people acquire a second dog, hoping it will provide company for the first. They might not realize that both dogs suffer deprivation when their humans are absent. The mischief of a single lonely pup is compounded when the whole pack gets involved. Nevertheless, the opposite can also hold true. That is, pack presence may act as a deterrent to loneliness activities like chewing, scratching, and barking.

Home-Alone Dogs

When left behind by their humans, dogs must call upon their own inner resources to weather the storm of separation. Waiting for alpha to return can be a grueling ordeal for some dogs. It's the same for the pack as the individual. Whenever you leave your pack, first provide food, exercise, and opportunity for all dogs to relieve themselves. Leaving dogs is a necessary part of life, so they have to deal with it and we must help them. Sometimes, home-alone dogs have behavioral problems caused by anxiety separation and boredom. There are pack parents who feel obsessed with guilt about their absences from home. Work, church, and other outings necessitate your absence. Dogs must learn to be home alone.

So, what do dogs do when humans are gone? Oh, my! They might do lots of things we wish they wouldn't! Take heart, though. As the pack matures, dogs usually settle down to sleep and dream when home alone. Provide for absences by giving your home-alone dogs plenty of diversionary toys. Teach them from the beginning to endure separation by practicing with short absences. Always crate young dogs when you're away. Leaving the whole pack loose invites problems, so don't do it unless your dogs are mature and well-seasoned in separation. In many places, there are specialized kennels that offer doggie day care. What could be better, if you can afford it? However, too much doggie day care and not enough separation training might backfire and actually complicate issues of loneliness and anxiety.

Diversionary toys help dogs endure loneliness and separation. One of the best is the Kong, which you can stuff with a little bit of peanut butter to occupy the dog for a while as it tries to disengage that delicious smelling treat. Don't put in too much peanut butter, however, since that can lead to stomach upsets, loose bowels, or vomiting. Moderation works best. To avoid having your dogs fight over them, crate each dog separately with several toys. If your pack can be safely left uncrated, leave sufficient diversions for them along with some duplicate toys as well. The following diversionary toys make great amusements for the home-alone pack:

- Gumabones
- Nylabones
- Raw marrow bones
- Safe stuffed toys (no removable parts that could be ingested)
- Dog biscuit or dry food
- Ice cubes in a bowl
- Radio or television playing at low volume

To Travel or Not to Travel: That Is the Question

How can you decide whether to take your dogs or not when you travel? Besides being a matter of personal taste, there are several points to consider, including these:

- Are you traveling alone or with companions? If you plan a trip with others, will they be amenable to having canines along on the journey? Explain to your travel companions the real needs your dogs will have traveling away from home so that if need be, they might suggest alternative plans. Not everyone who seems at first to be agreeable about traveling with dogs actually realizes how many extras are involved when animals share a journey. Will your travel companions be able to help with the dogs if necessary? If you're going away by yourself, you must make dog care arrangements just in case you become unable to take care of them yourself.
- Will dogs be permitted at the location to which you are traveling? This is the key issue to determine if you're thinking of taking the pack with you. Many dog-friendly resorts and lodgings

will be happy to have you and your dogs, but you should work out "permission" details before making a decision.

• How far away are you going and for how long? Dogs can adjust relatively well to new experiences. If they're permitted where you're going, the length of your stay and kind of accommodations available will help you decide if your dogs *really* should accompany you. (If you decide to leave them behind, keep in mind that length of stay and distance away from them will affect the plans you need to make for their care during your absence. Check carefully for safety provisions before you choose where to leave the pack.)

• Will you have sufficient time during your trip to accomodate your dogs with their daily routines, such as exercise, regular feeding schedules, and so on?

• What kind of transportation will be used for your trip, and is it dog friendly? Dogs have special needs when traveling. They can easily enjoy car trips, but they are not ordinarily allowed on trains. Flying dogs anywhere is a serious issue, and I'd rather not do it if it can be avoided. Dogs are not permitted to fly in extreme hot or cold weather. Flight accommodations are not always as safe or problem-free as flight carriers say they are. Do serious and careful investigating before finalizing transportation plans.

All these issues must be cleared up before you go anywhere with the pack!

Doggie Identification

When traveling with dogs—and even on local trips close to home—each member of the pack should have its own doggie identification tag. This should include the dog's name, your name, and telephone number. Such tags can be obtained from most pet shops, or you can make your own. I use large flat collars (in bright neon colors like hot pink), on which I print all the necessary information in fine point permanent marker.

Besides the I.D. on your dogs' collars, carry identification cards for each pet in your wallet or travel pack. These cards allow you to have more information available if needed than you can put on the basic identification tag dogs wear. They ensure against permanent loss of pets. The identification card should contain the following information:

- Photo of the dog
- Dog's breed or mix (as best as you can determine)
- Name of dog and home address
- Owner's name and telephone number (day and evening/weekend phone numbers, cell phone if you have one, and e-mail address)
- Veterinarian's name, address, and telephone number
- Name and telephone number of a responsible person to be contacted if you cannot care for your dogs for any reason

The Traveling Pack

If you decide one or more dogs will travel with you, the next step is to put together everything they need to be comfortable. Taking dogs along on a trip makes the whole experience different. While that difference might be totally positive, it can also become the source of problems along the way and at your destination. I have enjoyed many long automobile trips alone with my canine kids, so I'd never discourage pack parents from taking the dogs. As in everything else "dog," it is a matter of setting priorities. How much are you willing to give up to have your pack accompany you? Dogs are not commodities but sentient beings that deserve careful consideration in all our plans.

Your "travels with Charlie" might be camping trips, open road adventures, or distant vacations by plane or boat. Maybe you're making an overnight journey, and maybe you plan to stay a week or more in new surroundings. In any event, to share the excursion with your four-legged friends, follow these pointers for a happy trip:

- Plan ahead. Make reservations at lodgings that accept pets. State clearly to motel keepers that you plan to travel with more than one dog. Be honest in describing the size and character of your canine travel-mates.
- Prior to the trip, your veterinarian must examine the health of each canine traveler and give you written proof of health and current vaccinations.
- Place all the necessary canine papers in a travel pouch where you won't lose them and where you can find them as quickly as needed. Include a photo of each dog, with its name, breed type, current health certificate from the vet, proof of current vaccinations, and dog license.
- Each dog should wear an I.D. tag that also contains the dog's name, your name, address, phone number, and, if you plan to remain somewhere for a while, that address and phone number as well. It should also include the name and telephone number of your veterinarian and a responsible take-charge person who could assist the dogs in case anything unexpected happens to you. All this information won't fit on a simple dog tag, but the basics must be there, and the more that fits, the better, as long as it is legible.

- Before traveling, make sure your dogs will obey promptly and know their basic commands: come, sit, down, stay, quiet, wait, and so on. You can't wait until a week before travel time to teach them. It has to be a way of life with the pack, particularly if you hope they'll share some travel experiences with you.

- Pack sufficient food and fresh water from home for snack and drink stops along the way. Dogs easily get diarrhea from new water, so carry home water for them when traveling. Before you get to the end of the home water supply, begin to mix it with the local water available along the way or at your trip's destination so their stomachs can adjust gradually. Feed and water them at regular times.

- Plan your itinerary to include potty stops every couple of hours. Airplane travel does not accommodate dog plumbing, so exercise the pack sufficiently and allow plenty of elimination opportunities before boarding.

- Take along extra collars and leashes.

- Dogs are more relaxed with a blanket or comforter from home to sleep on in the car and at the motel, so pack a couple.

- Pack your pooper-scooper and plastic bags to clean up.

- Don't forget to include your pack's regular meds, vitamins, and heartworm or flea and tick medications needed for the trip. Avoid tick-infested areas during tick season.

- Include extra towels, blankets, baby wipes, combs and brushes, a first aid kit, and something to cover furniture where your dogs might alight at a lodging.

- Do *not* tranquilize pets for travel. It's not necessary and could be dangerous, regardless of what vets, breeders, or well-meaning friends might say.

How to Manage Dogs in the Car

Driving with dogs is second nature to me. I love having them on short road trips or long ones. I've driven up and down the east coast of the United States, from Maine to Florida, and it's always been a fantastic experience for my pack and me. I feel safe with my large German shepherds no matter what the hour or road conditions. Grabbing a little shuteye in a well-lit parking lot of an all-night restaurant under the watchful gaze of Grip, Geisty, and Cara Mia has always felt safe and secure. Driving through remote regions of northern Maine or in the Great Smokey Mountains of Tennessee and North Carolina, a woman alone, navigating a Dodge Grand Caravan with three furry co-pilots, was some of the best fun I've ever had.

Rules of the Road

Never take chances behind the wheel. From the first time you take your dogs into a vehicle, teach them how to travel safely in the car. Insist on their keeping the basic automobile safety rules for dogs. Your safety, the safety of other passengers, and the pack itself requires enforcement of the rules. Here they are:

- Dogs must sit or lie down still. Keep dogs unleashed in the vehicle.
- They are not allowed to fly back and forth over the seats. Carriers or crates made of strong, wire mesh with good ventilation are helpful in traveling with the pack.
- Doggie heads and body parts must remain inside the moving vehicle at all times, not out the window, and never in the rear of an open back vehicle.
- Dogs only exit from the back door or the side door, not

from the driver's door. (This is to keep dogs from being tempted to fly straight over the driver's head to get out of the car first.)

- Dogs must be leashed during pit stops at rest areas, and you must clean up after them, placing refuse in the proper receptacles.
- Dogs should never be permitted to annoy or interrupt other travelers, human or canine.

Pit Stops for the Pack

Certain absolutes never change when you live with dogs. The inevitable need for pit stops is one of them. Each and every journey must be punctuated with regular pit stops because dogs have to potty every few hours when riding in a vehicle. Motion seems to induce more frequent urinary needs. Take time to let your dogs stretch their legs and get some relief from being cramped in crate or car. The longer their confinement during the length of a trip, the greater their need for suitable regular relief breaks.

If you stop at sites that provide safe areas for dogs, you can let the pack run free for a little while, but only if there's no traffic hazard or the likelihood of encountering other animals and people. Many rest stops have large grassy fields or wooded places adjacent to puppy potty areas. Obey the signs. If free movement off lead is prohibited, walk your dogs briskly on lead before returning to your vehicle. Give them water and treats before resuming travel, but keep in mind that the more they drink, the more often they've got to stop.

A Serious Warning

Dogs overheat very rapidly in hot weather. The danger of canine death lurks in every vehicle because of overheating. *Never*, under any conditions, leave dogs unattended in a closed vehicle. *Never.* Even in seventy-degree weather, which seems not to be dangerous, car interiors heat up quickly. Internal temperatures may soar way past outdoor temperatures in a short period of time. Dogs can succumb to heat prostration and death in a matter of minutes.

Even if you leave the windows open only a little bit, your dogs are still at grave risk. Internal air cannot circulate properly in vehicles, even with windows slightly open, so heat builds up. Many dogs die every year as a result of tragic accidents caused by owners who inadvertently leave them in poorly ventilated places, vehicles, or other close quarters. Heat stroke is an awful catastrophe that takes only a short period of time and could usually have been avoided. Don't give heat stroke the opportunity to slay your beloved pets.

Dogs can also freeze to death easily in cold weather. Don't presume that canine fur keeps them sufficiently warm when temperatures drop below freezing. People who leave dogs in vehicles on cold winter nights while they sleep in cozy motel rooms can be sadly shocked to find their canine counterparts frozen to death at dawn. Small amounts of human negligence have claimed many a life of innocent pets.

Check for safety whenever you stop. An area might *look* safe, but since you're just passing through, you can't really know for sure. Never rely on looks alone. Leaving pets in an insecure and unknown place invites tragedy. Unscrupulous people steal dogs of all breeds, every size, shape, and age, even large working dogs. The tragic victims of canine kidnapping are often sold into experimentation or abused and killed. Some are stolen for resale or placed in new ownerships by thieves without conscience. Think ahead to provide everything you need for your trip so you won't have to leave your pack unattended in your quest for forgotten items or food. If you *must* stop to eat, park where you can see your vehicle. Lock it, but only if outside temperatures are safe and there's no danger of dogs overheating or freezing. Pick up the food and bring it back to your car so your animals won't need to be left alone for long.

How to Manage Your Dogs at a Motel

One of the most memorable trips I took with my pack of German shepherds was a journey to Quebec for the Canadian National Dog Show. It's a long drive from Brooklyn to Quebec and we had great adventures all along the way. Dogs are conversation pieces. I met truckers and families at every pit stop who commented on the beauty and strength of my wonderful pack, so conversation flowed easily, and the dogs loved greeting new people. I enjoyed sharing dog stories with other dog owners en route. Our journey home was equally delightful. We stopped overnight at a small motel high in the Adirondacks, where I had detoured to do some scenic photography. We were graciously accommodated in a cabin furthest back on the property so my dogs would not be a problem for others. The motel was fenced in with deep woods all around it. There the dogs enjoyed a long run before we boarded again and hit the road.

Motels that accept canine guests don't usually charge additional security for them, but if you have failed to make reservations in advance, you might find yourself unable to locate a dog-friendly motel. Explain your situation, and offer the motel keeper an additional amount as assurance that your dogs will not cause any damage. Some will accommodate you under those conditions, and others will not. It's the luck of the draw if you don't make prior arrangements. I've always found people to be reasonably helpful, even if, as a general rule, pets were not wanted.

Motel Manners

Keep these motel tips in mind:

- Request a ground-floor room so nighttime bathroom trips outdoors will be easier for you, the dogs, and other guests.
- Ask the motel keeper where your dogs can "do business," and clean up afterward.
- Never permit dogs to climb up on beds, chairs, or other furniture unless you first cover them with an old sheet from home.
- Never allow dogs to drink from toilets, particularly outside your home where you have no idea what kind of cleaning solutions were applied. Some are poisonous.
- Put dog food and water bowls in the bathroom where floors are tiled to avoid damaging spills to the carpet.
- Keep dogs leashed coming and going from your accommodation.
- Never permit barking or noisy roughhousing at the motel, inside or out. Prevent your dogs from getting revved up and disturbing others.
- If a canine accident causes damage, go immediately to the motel keeper to report it and offer to pay whatever is necessary.
- Keep the pack under control at all times.

Between forty and sixty million dog owners travel with their pets every year. The motel industry is increasingly accommodating to animal lovers who want to take their dogs along. Recent years have also seen an expansion in pet-friendly lodgings, such as campsites. Human responsibility for animals will ensure their continued acceptance in the future.

Dogs in Flight

I wish dogs never had to fly in airplanes, but since they do, this section deals with one of the most difficult methods of canine travel: flight. Flying is fearful. Dog owners prefer not to send their pets on airplanes because of too many sad endings, accidents, injuries, deaths, and losses that have taken place through the years. While it's true that pets in flight can be insured, what good is financial reimbursement in exchange for the life of a beloved canine companion? Pack travel by plane is even riskier.

If you *must* fly your dogs, make early reservations because airline availability for dogs is limited. You might be very disappointed if you wait till the last minute. Pet accommodations are sparse to begin with, and it's actually rather unlikely that your whole pack can make an airplane trip together. There's no discount for bulk, and flying is expensive. If there's not sufficient space on board, you'll have to decide which dogs accompany you and which ones stay home.

Pet owners are rightly wary of airplane travel. Under the best of circumstances, my advice to dog people is not to fly pets. Don't subject them to the dangers and vicissitudes of air travel if it can possibly be avoided.

Not every dog in flight perishes at the hands of a negligent or rushed airline attendant. Many dogs survive plane trips, disembarking in good shape and eagerly bounding forth from their crates into the loving arms of doting owners. Breeders frequently air ship animals cross-country and across the world. Dogs older than eight weeks make successful air journeys to their new homes, no worse for the wear. But if air travel is the only way to go for an *optional* vacation, maybe the wisest thing is not to go at all. At least, not the dog. It's up to you.

Small and medium-sized dogs can ride in carriers that fit under the passenger's seat in the cabin section of the plane, but larger dogs must be transported in cargo. Therein lies the rub. Airline carriers have specific policies about pet travel. Some only accept small dogs for in-cabin flight (and their definition of small may be much smaller than you expect). Unfortunately, all other dogs are dispatched to cargo, where a number of variables are potential hazards to their health and safety. If you absolutely *must* ship your dogs in cargo, check out the qualifications of the airline first. Find out the policies and procedures of the air carrier you select, and get the name of someone in charge of animal shipping so you'll have a real contact person if you need one.

An airline that is a professional pet shipper should be used to make sure the dogs arrive safely. Only transport dogs in a cargo hold that is safe enough for humans to ride in. Find out if that's the case before you commit your dogs to travel in such a place. The decision is yours, but these are the facts.

A federal law enacted in 2002, the Safe Air Travel for Animals Act, requires that airline and baggage personnel receive special training in the proper handling and care of animals during air transport. That doesn't mean that such persons will necessarily be conscientiously concerned about the welfare of traveling pets. This law, however, requires a separate reporting system to be created by airlines for reporting animals that are lost, injured, or killed. It demands that remedial measures be put in place to address and prevent future life-threatening accidents. The liability coverage airlines face because of this law has been increased. But what you see is not always what you get. It takes the serious commitment of airline management to make sure these laws are enforced and to require personnel to carry out *all* of their obligations when handling animal cargo. In the past, some airlines avoided facing the legal provisions for pet safety in flight by simply disallowing pets in cargo.

To ship animals by air carrier, outside temperatures at the flight's starting point and destination must be moderate, not extreme. Find out if weather conditions are suitable. If they're not and if it's too hot or too cold for dogs to fly safely, most airlines will not accept them for flight. Weather conditions change, but the hottest and coldest months of the year are notoriously harsh for animals who have to fly.

Rules of the Air

These regulations must be kept to send pets by air:

- Dogs must be at least eight weeks of age to travel by plane.
- They must be in good health.
- Pregnant or lactating bitches should not be shipped.
- Observe animal quarantines at point of arrival.
- Choose direct, nonstop flights if you can.
- Morning or evening travel is preferable.
- Avoid holidays and special weekends, when airlines are particularly busy.
- Before flight, obtain proper veterinary checkups, health certificates, and proof of current vaccinations.
- Do not use tranquilizers. Do not sedate.
- Exercise dogs before feeding and before flight time.

- Give food and water within four hours of flight time, but do not overfeed.
- Do not give toys or chewables during flight.
- Use buckle-type collars on dogs, and be sure there are no tags or possible parts that could get caught in the crate during flight. Make a little cloth sleeve for tags to prevent snagging.
- Carry your dog's leash. Do not put a leash into the crate because that would pose a safety hazard. You can also attach it outside the crate.
- Use an airline-approved travel kennel with your pet's name on the outside, clearly marked, adequate ventilation openings, and sufficient interior space for the dog to stand, turn, sit or lie down comfortably. Be sure a label saying LIVE ANIMALS is affixed for appropriate visibility and arrows to indicate the top of the kennel.

The airline kennel must also have the name and address with telephone number of an individual who can be contacted at the point of destination if necessary. Put absorbent bedding, such as newspaper or a blanket, inside the travel kennel in case your dog has an accident. An empty food and water dish should be inside the kennel so the dog can be taken care of if there are delays in transit. Tape important paperwork to the top of the animal flight crate, having first inserted the papers into a plastic bag to avoid damage. (Keep a second copy of all paperwork in your baggage or purse.) When dogs arrive at their destination, they're mighty eager to get out of their crates, so be prepared for a quick exit. Remove them from their crates in a safe spot away from traffic since they will be excited and anxious to get out of confinement.

There is separate legislation regarding air travel for assistance service dogs, such as guide dogs for the blind, dogs that assist the hearing impaired, and dogs for the disabled. The law allows these animals to travel in the cabin with their person. The International Association of Assistance Dog Partners provides detailed information about service dogs at their Web site, *www.iaadp.org*. If you travel with an assistance dog, you have the right to priority seating and space accommodations for your canine partner, but the Department of Transportation doesn't make airlines provide this additional space free of charge, nor can it force an airline to require the person sitting next to a disabled individual to yield floor space for the comfort of the assistance dog.

There are numerous conditions for flight travel with service dogs. Check them out online, or write to the IAADP. I am mentioning this, not only to be of assistance to persons with service dogs, but also to advise others, lest they be tempted to sneak a furry friend onboard as an assistance dog, as one multi-dog owner recently suggested. Flight attendants will demand evidence that your dog is not a pet but a worker. So if you're thinking of getting a guide dog harness just for effect, or a backpack, vest, or cape that is the uniform of a service dog, be prepared to describe in detail the service your dog is trained to do—and don't be surprised if you are asked to demonstrate the training.

Bon Voyage

So, there you have it! Tips for traveling with the pooches you love. Bon voyage! May Saint Christopher and Saint Francis of Assisi, the universal patrons of folks that love animals, guide you and your mutts through happy trails. We turn our focus now to those left behind.

Boarding Kennels

When all the alternatives have been considered, you might decide to leave the whole pack behind or just some of its members. Dogs can be cared for at home during owner absence if reliable, trustworthy help is available. You need a capable pet sitter to visit your home at least twice, but preferably several times a day, while you're away. Besides getting out to relieve themselves, dogs need food, exercise, and human contact. The home-care pet sitter should also wash the dog dishes, provide fresh water daily, and clean up any messes that might happen. The advantage of leaving dogs in their own homes is their familiarity with surroundings so they won't go through place anxiety along with separation anxiety.

Boarding dogs in a professional boarding kennel is the second alternative. First, find a reputable boarding kennel, and check it out thoroughly. By making inquiries and checking references, you can contact others who used the facility satisfactorily. Visit the boarding kennel before leaving your dogs there. Try to meet the attendants who will take care of them.

Selection Criteria for Boarding Kennels

Good boarding kennels pass these selection criteria:

- Clean, safe environment with adequate staff in attendance
- Well-ventilated and well-lit kennel area
- Separation of dogs from cats and from each other, except for specific request by owners to board pack members together
- Ability and willingness of staff to follow feeding or medicine distribution as close to your home schedule as possible

- Provision for sufficient hours of outdoor time and exercise in a safe, fenced-in area
- Veterinary assistance or emergency service available if needed
- Kindness of manner in the way attendants handle boarders
- A professional environment from entry to exit
- References made available on demand
- Reasonable pricing

Home-boarding is also available in many cities and towns and should fit the criteria (above) for regular boarding kennels. Visit the site where your dogs will be kept before placing them in anyone's care.

When you leave dogs with a professional home-boarding manager or in a kennel, exchange all the information necessary for you and the caregiver to stay in touch during your absence. If you have concerns, put them forward, and have them addressed before you leave your dogs. Reputable boarding kennels will be glad to give you a tour in advance of placement. Some allow pets to visit beforehand or make day care arrangements so the dogs can get used to the environment and the people.

Talk to the Dogs and They Will Tell You

No one appreciates the very special genius
of your conversation as the dog does.
—Christopher Morley

Living with dogs has taught me many things, not only about me and them but also about the universe, the mystery of being, ineffable realities of the world beyond the senses, and the inexplicable and eternal truths that lie on the other side of everything the mind can comprehend or word and thought communicate. In the stillness of long predawn walks with my pack along the Atlantic beach at Far Rockaway or through silent, night vigils in a deep pine forest at Athens, Maine, walking and talking with dogs has been a school for living. The human-canine bond forged in fun and games, training, and work, is deepened by the ultimate connection that is a sharing of silence, separate and apart from the noise of everyday life. Spending time in meditation surrounded by my dogs has been a spiritual journey inward for which I am deeply grateful.

The mystical connection we share with all the rest of life exists beyond the boundaries of time and space. It's not a matter of opinion or bias. It simply is. This connection is not determined by one's religious faith or lack of such, but goes instead to the heart of human experience. It does not require theological explanations, nor is it rooted in any specific creed. It is the interconnectedness of all things, beyond language or imagination, a portal between species that simply *is*.

Some will think there cannot be intelligent communication

except among humans. Others who have experienced something more will not need to prove it, but will rest assured that what they have touched and seen and heard is a real connection between species that transcends explanations and requires no justification. It just *is*. The longer I live with animals, the more I realize the power of such experiences as lie within the reach of all, available only to those who can shed prejudice and preconceptions, becoming open and ready to observe and to learn. Coming from a Judaeo-Christian tradition, I find words of wisdom from the Book of Job in the Old Testament to ring true of my bond with animals:

> . . . ask the beasts, and they will instruct you; the birds of the air, and they will tell you; or the plants of the earth, and they will teach you; and the fish of the sea will declare unto you. Who among all these does not know that the hand of the LORD has done this? And in his hand is the life of every living thing and the breath of all mankind.
>
> Job 12: 7–10

All spiritual traditions, East and West, absent none, contain concepts that are essentially the same: reverence for all creation, the interconnectedness of all things, the unity of the universe, the bond between species—what the Buddhist monk-teacher Thich Nhat Han calls "interbeing."

Our lives are enriched because we share them with the pack. Dogs are so attuned to us that even without speech they are totally capable of understanding us and, in return, of making themselves understood. The first step toward "hearing" what your dogs have to say involves doing a little bit of mental housecleaning.

The human mind, referred to adeptly in Buddhist thought as "monkey mind," is always chattering, swinging wildly from one thought to another, darting to and fro through an avalanche of ideas. With all this noise going on inside of us, we might easily miss what our animals are trying to say. Mental housecleaning is about getting rid of internal noise. Our monkey mind must be stilled so that we can pay attention to what really matters. The open, honest mind is fertile for communication with the pack.

Verbal language is not the only way people speak to one another. We communicate through art, photography, drawings, paintings, music, laughter, weeping, signs, and body language. It is just the same with animals. Theirs is a language of pictures, sounds, smells, and feelings, a universal language that belongs to all species, theirs and ours. If you want to tap into it, you must first get rid of the garbage in your head.

Cast out the preoccupations of worry and endless plans, procrastinations, prognostications, noise, and chatter that clog the brain and burden the heart. When you go into that rarefied atmosphere of inner cleanliness and reduced static, you will be much more kindly disposed toward dogs and other beings that prowl the parameters of your reality, ever hopeful of engaging you in their world and rescuing you, as it were, from yours. The interbeing we share with all creatures that inhabit this earth of ours is a richness that can only be appreciated by those who take time to ponder it with reverence and respect.

So far, I have not meant animal communication as done by professionals capable of authentic interspecies conversation. Up to this point I have been referring to the contemplative and spiritual dimension of our life with animals. Simple people like you and me, ordinary folks, untrained as animal translators, can listen to and speak with our dogs in the intimacy of our lives, quietly and at home wherever we are, no fuss, no show, just talking together. This communication is nonverbal but direct. Most dog owners have felt the wonderment of suddenly knowing what's on the dog's mind or the delight in realizing your dog understands what you're talking about.

Talking Dog

To be honest with you, I do engage in a little dog-talk now and again. I growl, yodel, yelp, howl, and make other sounds that are more appropriate to wolves and canines than to people. Or, so one would think. The response I get in my effort to talk dog led me to investigate the way canines communicate. In his studies of animal language, Fred H. Harrington, then associate professor of psychology at Mt. St. Vincent University in Halifax, Nova Scotia, created a marvelous tape recording of wolf vocalizations. He had been tracking wolf communication since 1971. The tape Harrington made was produced by the Science Museum of Minnesota and released in 1986. Since then I have listened to it repeatedly. It is awesome to hear the voices of these wolves just the way they sound in the wild. Harrington's recordings were made in the totally natural conditions of the Superior National Forest of Minnesota. My interest in wolves was based on the natural similarities dogs have with them. The wolf tape paved the way for me to learn dog-talk.

Harrington followed the development of howling during a wolf's first year of life, the most important time of learning about its environment, its place in the pack, and how to communicate with its elders and peers. He observed and listened, studying the pack intently, until he could understand what the various intonations might mean. The long howl of a lone wolf calling its packmates is an unforgettable sound. Remember the wolves in the film *Dr. Zhivago?* That piercing voice in the wilderness just never leaves your mind. I played Harrington's tape for my pack when Grip was a young puppy. My older female, Cara Mia, was lying on the couch listening. She began to croon softly when she heard the young puppy wolves whine and whimper in their den, clearly trying to answer them. The same night, as we continued to listen to the tape in our darkened living room, young Grip, less than a year old, stood up and stuck out his powerful still-developing chest, lifted his head upwards and stretched his throat to utter a howl that thrilled me to the bottom of my soul. Grip truly answered the voice of the wolf on that tape and sounded like a wolf himself.

In the days and weeks that followed, I carried a small tape recorder to the beach and to an evergreen scrub forest at Old Fort Tilden near Breezy Point. As we walked on long treks in the darkness, my pack and I, we played Harrington's tape. Inevitably, in each environment, whether in my cozy living room in Park Slope or on the lonely beach and dune at Old Fort Tilden, my dogs, civilized city canines, howled and echoed word after word of the wolf pack on the tape. Thank you, Fred H. Harrington, wherever you are. In many years with dogs, I have come to recognize some primitive sounds that seem reflective of the vocalizations of wolves. Consulting the interpretations of Fred Harrington about the likely meanings of wolf howling, I have sought understanding as I wondered about the link between one species and another.

Understanding Wolf Talk

Harrington said howls can be any of the following:

- An adult wolf calling for packmates or for a sexual partner
- Whining of a puppy wolf trying to free itself from entanglement in the den
- Moan of contentment from feeding pups
- Young wolves crying for their mother, who has left the den in search of food
- Bark howling of adult wolves rallying to the defense of the den against intruders
- Hungry eager howls of young wolves when adults are returning to them with food
- Communal howling of the pack to cement group bonds or to ward off strangers from approaching
- Single howl to identify one's location, which is made by wolves individually in response to some kind of wolf roll call

As wolf puppies grow, they gain confidence in their deepening voices and learn to participate in pack life using their wolf howl language to communicate with one another. Eventually, they develop a full repertoire of sounds, including the deep, strong, long howls of adult wolves. I was just building my first dog pack when I came upon this fascinating information. It seemed so appropriate. When I heard the incredible responses my dogs made to the wolf pack, I realized irrevocably how linked we are with the past. I thought about their wolf ancestors who first entered the caves of early humans, never to leave man's side again. I imitated the sounds on Harrington's tape and delighted in my little pack's expanded vocalizations as Grip and Cara Mia tried to reply. Not everybody wants to talk wolf or dog, that's for sure, but it's interesting to note that language is a universal yearning among animals as well as people. It's the desire to communicate.

Listening to Canine Chatter

By paying attention to the pack, we soon realize there's quite a bit of canine chatter going on. Some of it is vocal—yelps, barks, whines, and growls—and some of it is body language. Dogs shove and muscle their way into the center of the pack, particularly if *you're* there with food treats. The rough and tumble play of dogs is another form of canine chatter. The more you bark and growl at your dogs, imitating their sounds, the more they'll vocalize for you. The natural culmination of this exchange is for dogs to speak on command and reduce their voices to a whisper when told to do so. All the members of my pack, past and present, are talkers. I've encouraged this by trying to communicate in dog-wolf lingo myself. Dogs can never master human language, but the language of dog is something you and I can much more fully appreciate and comprehend.

The Mystical Side of Human-Canine Interaction

We can't explain all the nuances we experience with our dogs, but more than a few pack people have shared with me amazing and incredible experiences of connectedness with their canine friends. We will speak of telepathic animal communication later in this chapter. What I am referring to here is a deep connectedness with dogs, in which we feel the transfer of powerful energy, a mighty rhythm that moves through pack and people. Beyond the shadow of a doubt, when we experience this, we know something magnificent is going on.

A commonplace, less mystical example is the unexplainable way dogs seem to know in advance where we're going. They're at the door, ready to move, before we even put our shoes on. It's no coincidence that when it's time to go home to them after work, we feel some awakened mental contact with our waiting pets although still separated by miles. Dogs have let people know when a seizure was about to happen to them. They warn their families about home fires and explosions. They lead them safely out of danger, sometimes before it even happens! Why? How? What makes the pack so amazingly aware?

Grieving humans report that their dogs seem to have an uncanny understanding of their loss and ability to share their pain. Two years ago I was a pallbearer for my dad. Abby, my German shepherd, walked by my side as we carried Poppie to his lasting resting place, she and I, the only females bearing our precious burden with several nephews and friends. What a privilege was ours! We stood together near the coffin as it was sprinkled with holy water amid prayers and incense. Abby's attitude was deeply perceptive. My grief was hers. Was it because my dad loved dogs so much? Was it just the contagion of my own feelings? Did Abby, indeed, realize she had lost our best friend?

Dad had an enormous sense of humor, so I'm sure he would have appreciated the fleeting thought I had standing there. I realized that Abby was looking down into the grave, such a huge hole in the earth from a dog's point of view. Perhaps she was remembering Grip, her recently deceased buddy, the world's most avid hole digger! In my grief I had to smile, as I imagined Abby must be thinking: "Oh, Grip, what a *fantastic hole* for burying bones!"

Dogs give us their sympathy and unconditional love through every phase of our lives, but nothing is more awesome than sharing fear, grief, and other really deep emotions with the pack. Far from being unintelligent, dogs communicate their understanding and concern in ways that go beyond human language.

When I pray and meditate, my dogs are always with me, staying close and silent as if they know what's going on. I light the candles before my icons, and the pack grows quiet and still, making no demands on me nor interrupting or impinging on my solitude. They are simply *there*. My dogs have always accompanied me on my spiritual journey, fellow travelers caught up together in the mystery of Ultimate Reality.

We can hear the echo of our own interbeing with all creatures by reflecting on these words from the 27th verse of Chapter 13 *Bhagavad-Gita, The Song of God*, one of India's most sacred scriptures: "He sees truly who sees the Supreme Lord abiding in all beings, the immortal within the mortal." Our connection to the pack is manifestation of the Supreme Lord abiding there as in all beings. All things are one, and we are part of that oneness.

Mystical experience is about entering the deepest dimensions of reality, a profound opening up of human awareness. Enlightenment means seeing reality as it actually is, cutting through the encumbrances of human fabrication, letting go of emotional baggage and intellectual pride. That's what happiness is all about, and that's the definition of enlightenment, yours and mine for the taking.

Wisdom permeates all time, all peoples, every race, creed, and nationality. It transcends personal opinions and intellectual differences. Mystics and holy people from every tradition, once they have seen the Light, transcend dogma and seem to agree about the things that matter most. The sacred truth that lies within all things in the core of reality is there for us to encounter and experience, too. The same wholeness and harmony that unites the galaxies, planets, earth, animal and plant kingdoms, a living, breathing life force that pulses everywhere and beats within the heartbeat of our own dear pack. Let your dogs show you. We might search the world for happiness, but the miracle is right inside of us. It's all one thing. Everything fits. Everything belongs. Right here. Right now. Pack life has taught me this through many years of living with dogs.

Dogs' incorruptible nature is exactly what it's meant to be, no more and no less. There's no encrustation of falsehood, deception, vanity, or lies. Dogs don't cheat. They give us exactly what they are. The fullness of dogness lies in each and every one of them, mutts or champions. Dogs are a truth that stands whole and complete, needing no alteration. Don't you wish we could also be the same? Completely incorruptible, totally without falsehood, deception, vanity or lies? Living with the pack gives us plenty of daily opportunities to face ourselves and become more and more true to our own reality as they are to theirs. The hidden mystery at the heart of all creation is how and why it all came to be in the first place, so perfect, so diverse. There's no junk in God's making. There are no junk dogs, either. Mixed breeds, mutts and mongrels, purebreds of every kind, they are all *perfect beings*. The so-called faults and flaws attributed to certain dogs by breed clubs are just about manmade standards. They have to do with external perception, appearances. They have nothing to do with the essential wholeness and worth of the tiniest puppy, such as it is. Living with the pack can open your eyes to spiritual insights and realizations that heal and lead to happiness. Pack life can show us how deeply everything is interrelated, connected, harmonious and whole. Realizing this, we can rid ourselves of alienation, loneliness, desperation, and isolation. All things are one, and we are part of the same oneness.

Animal Communicators and the Pack

There's yet another layer to this onion, so let's peel away! My earliest encounters with animal communicators found me quite a skeptic with little interest in the topic, disbelieving what others tried to tell me. Experience, the best teacher, gradually led me in the opposite direction. You can think what you will about the likelihood that animals and people can share telepathic connections, but from the vantage point of personal experience, I'd still like to share some thoughts with you. Accept or reject them as you see fit, but have an open mind. They stand out there just the way they happened, no exaggeration, no myth.

A couple of years after my German shepherd, Geisty, produced a beautiful litter of seven puppies in the autumn of 1995, I wanted to breed her one more time and keep a puppy for my pack. I took Geisty to a magnificent male German shepherd, named Degen, that I liked a lot. Degen was a champion belonging to my friend Dottie Seuter. Dottie had established herself and Degen as an outstanding Schutzhund sport team, and Degen's pedigree was impeccable. I knew his bloodlines would be a good match with Geisty's, so we arranged a breeding. Geisty, in the pink of heat, flagged and flirted with Degen but refused to stand for breeding, though her time was right. Degen never sired puppies with Geisty.

That day, discouraged because I really wanted this litter, I prepared to go home carrying my heavy load of disappointment. Two breeder friends present with Dottie and me that day suggested that I consult an animal communicator they knew, Marlene Sandler, whose reputation is well-founded in the field of interspecies telepathic communication. But I didn't know Marlene at all, and my skepticism kept trying to find ways to avoid meeting her. I was not a believer! My friends kept insisting that Marlene could tell me a lot more about Geisty than I could know about her on my own.

My good old-fashioned Italian Catholic upbringing never prepared me for the inscrutable experience of animal communication that Marlene Sandler demonstrated. After hemming and hawing and making jokes about it, my friends prevailed. I made an appointment to speak with Marlene Sandler, the animal communicator—that is, to have Marlene Sandler speak with Geisty about the unsuccessful breeding.

Marlene Sandler *did* speak with Geisty, and Geisty spoke with her through mental telepathy. I wouldn't have believed it at all, except that here was this stranger sitting at her telephone in Warrington, Pennsylvania telling me things about my life with Geisty miles away in Brooklyn, New York—things that even my close friends didn't know. Geisty, dear soul that she was (blabbermouth!), had no particular interest in revealing the intimate secrets of her sex life or why she had rejected Degen, but delighted instead, in telling Marlene Sandler all about me and my dogs, as well as facts like her back injury at six months of age while engaging in rough-and-tumble play with Cara Mia and Grip. Yes, young Geisty had run headlong into a wrought iron fence in the Prospect Park playground. The impact had thrown her up in the air, and as I remembered this clearly, cued by the psychic's reference to it, I started to speak excitedly. Marlene Sandler finished the story herself, saying: "Geisty landed on her left side and you thought she was dead!"

Geisty's old back injury made it uncomfortable for her to be mounted by the male during breeding. How did Marlene know about that accident? Further along in the conversation, Geisty told the animal communicator that she loved sleeping on the blue thing! What blue thing? The blue thing was a blue sheet I had spread over the futon in my living room, formerly Cara

Mia's favorite perch, but after her death, Geisty's personal place of honor from which she could view the entire apartment.

What made Marlene Sandler say to me that she knew I didn't have much gold in my apartment, only the gold on the icons and icon lampada that hold candles in front of the icons? Geisty told her. I wouldn't have brought it up. Marlene said, "Geisty loves gold. Get her a golden neckerchief."

The thing that forced me to reconsider my attitude toward telepathic communication with animals was when Marlene Sandler asked me if I had a bright colored sport utility vehicle. She had correctly identified visually my red Toyota Tercel hatchback, which looked like a typical SUV, though much smaller. Marlene astonished me by saying, "Geisty loved that car." She went on to state a genuine historic fact that she couldn't have fabricated. "Yes," she said, without missing a beat, "Geisty loved that car because she rode in the front seat with you." It was absolutely true. I never put Geisty in the back of the hatchback when she was a puppy because she was so tiny that I feared my larger dogs, Cara Mia and Grip, might overpower her or crush her if the car stopped suddenly. She loved riding up front and always tried to keep her front seat priority as the years went on. Marlene Sandler knew all about it from Geisty's point of view!

During that incredible conversation with Marlene Sandler, Geisty revealed through the psychic things that only she and I could know about our life together. She even told the animal communicator that she wanted her stainless steel dining bowl washed after every meal and that licking did not suffice. What a little tattletale! My experience with Marlene Sandler and Geisty made me realize there's something incredibly marvelous but *very real* about interspecies communication. It made the hair on the back of my neck stand up straight.

Marlene Sandler simply couldn't possibly have known about the things she said during her communication with Geisty. She didn't know me. She had never visited my home. She had never seen my vehicle. She was a total stranger to me and my dogs. Nevertheless, with only the telephone connecting us, Marlene spoke telepathically with my dog.

I did some research about her afterwards and found out that Marlene Sandler's work with animals is very well known. She gives workshops, lectures, and consultations. She is a Reiki healer and works with a wide range of holistic professionals, using her specific telepathic skills to uncover health and behavior problems and help solve them. You can reach Marlene Sandler at (215) 491-0707. She and others in her field offer animal lovers a whole new way of understanding their pets.

I saw my dog in real time, and Marlene saw her telepathically. Geisty told her own story through images and feelings shared across the distance. Yes, I would have continued to doubt the veracity of telepathic interspecies communication had I not experienced Marlene Sandler's incredible skill. At that time, I was writing about God and dogs for magazines and journals in the United States and Canada. Some of my essays focused on spirituality while others were about raising and training dogs. After my encounter with Marlene, I collected information and interviews with other interspecies communicators. I contacted many animal psychics to learn how they became involved in this work. My intention was to write an article about animal communicators, but I allowed myself to be dissuaded from doing so by a friend of mine who was a German breeder and tough skeptic. He feared I would lose credibility as a dog writer if I pursued this topic and strongly advised me against it. I folded and let the idea go at that time, keeping the dossier I had built.

Now, a few years later, the whole thing has come of age, and knowledgeable professionals no longer regard it as quackery. Instead, they recognize that something big is opening up here, a portal to new ways of dealing with animals, finding out what their issues are, and helping them. Telepathy is the transmission of feeling across distance. It embraces the psyche or soul of an individual, human and animal. It touches the spirit within.

Animal communicators translate the mental pictures and feelings of animals that they receive telepathically. They can elicit information from animals about their emotional distress or physical problems. Animal psychics, as they are often called, can assist animals with trauma, fear, grief, loss, loneliness, and confusion. The finely honed skills of a genuine animal communicator can help you understand what's going on with your pets in a compassionate, nonjudgmental way.

The Place of Music in Pack Life

Living with dogs is a wonderful experience. Learning to speak their language is amazing and awesome. With our packs, we can participate in the sacred journeys of the shamans following our animals into their world as they have followed us into ours. Music, too, is a language that speaks to everyone, including our dogs. They are amazingly responsive to harmonic sound.

Music has a salutary effect on the pack. It is soothing and calming. It can allay frustration, loneliness, and pain. From young whelps to venerable aging canines, I have seen my dogs and others respond positively to music. Many dog breeders pipe classical music into kennel areas, especially their whelping rooms and puppy care areas. Soft, peaceful music makes a better environment for pets and people. Dogs left alone for long periods of time do better when there's music nearby. You can often see this in their facial expressions when you watch dogs exposed to pleasing music. Music should have a definite place in our lives and that of our dogs. Try it. You'll see its usefulness for the pack. If you haven't tried using music with your pack yet, let me tell you, it's very helpful in the multi-dog environment. Dogs innately respond to rhythm and harmonic sound. They get excited with peppy music and calm with that which is serene. My dogs behave best in the car, for example, when there's music playing on the radio. They settle down quietly at home as soon as I put on the music, and why not? Sentient beings respond to rhyme, rhythm, and song. It's just in the nature of reality that everything fits together as it does.

Chapter 12

Emergencies in the Pack

He who is cruel to animals becomes hard also in his dealings with men. We can judge the heart of a man by his treatment of animals.

—Immanuel Kant

I hope you never need any of the information presented in this chapter, but given the exigencies of life, accidents do happen, emergencies arise, and the better part of wisdom is to be prepared in advance. It's hard enough to handle one dog properly in an emergency, but taking care of the pack is even more challenging when trouble strikes. Even the most rudimentary knowledge of how to deal with canine emergencies could help you save lives. And even a little knowledge is better than no knowledge when it comes to dealing with freak accidents and emergency situations. The more you know, however, the greater chance you'll be able to stay calm and effectively work through the crisis.

When you read the words, "Stay calm", you might think this requirement is so self-evident, why should we bother talking about it at all? According to statistics for 2002, approximately 62 percent of American households have pets. Of that number, about 40 million homes have dogs, frequently more than one. There are nearly 70 million dogs on record in American homes, and those are only the ones that were counted! You can easily imagine the frequency with which dog emergencies occur, and the fact of the matter is that many people just go ballistic when something unexpected happens to their canine kids. Truth be told, keeping calm doesn't come naturally. One has to develop a lifestyle of calmness if one hopes to remain so under severe stress.

On the other hand, you might say, "Hey, look! I have a pack of canines. I live with stress." Surely, we do. All the more must we strive to be calm and compassionate. In the heat of the moment, we need nerves of steel and hearts of gold. Compassionate calm brings people through emergencies and is the best chance of survival for all involved.

Distinguishing Emergencies from ordinary Troubles

Many kinds of emergency situations can arise in the life of your pack. In the best of worlds, you wouldn't have to face them, or at least, not most of them, but life being what it is, you'll meet your fair share of emergencies over the years. Your ability to handle them depends on understandings and knowledge acquired *before* they happen!

Canine Emergencies

Since September 11, we are all much more conscious of disaster, much more aware of the potential for terrible unexpected things to happen. Daily life changed forever that day. It made me realize as nothing else has that life is fragile and fraught with urgency and impermanence. But even if the terrorist attacks of that day had never happened, knowing what to do in an emergency is just as critical. To reduce the risk of pet loss in the confusion of an emergency, keep these important things in mind. Besides national disasters and local events like fires and accidents, there are also canine-specific emergencies that claim hundreds of lives every year.

The Most Serious Emergencies

The following list names a few that you should know about if you have animals, especially if you have a pack:

- Bloat or gastric torsion
- Dogs getting hit by a car
- Broken bones
- Wounds
- Excessive bleeding
- Foreign bodies in eyes, nose, and other orifices

- Swallowing foreign bodies
- Poisoning
- Bites and stings from bees, wasps, and other insects
- Dogs biting people
- Dogs fighting dogs
- Heat stroke and exhaustion
- Hypothermia and frostbite
- Burns
- Holiday disasters
- Terrorism and natural disasters

Got the picture? Unfortunately, there's plenty of stuff out there that pack parents can worry about. On the other hand, you can become acquainted with some of the many sources of information available and try to assimilate useful knowledge to help prevent panic when one or more members of the pack faces an emergency. A book like this is not intended to give extensive information on this topic or detailed procedures for dealing with all the emergencies listed above, but at least we can bring your attention to these important issues. It will be up to you to seek additional information, and there's plenty available, online and in books and articles readily accessible.

Times When Veterinary Consultations Are Urgent

Call your veterinarian right away if you notice any of the following:

- Your dog has wounds that expose bone.
- Your dog is bleeding profusely from a wound or from its mouth.
- Your dog has a fever (temperature higher than 104°F).
- Your dog cannot move.

- Your dog has an eye injury or appears to be blind.
- Your dog is having great difficulty urinating or defecating.
- Your dog has profuse diarrhea or vomiting.
- Your dog is in shock.
- Your dog is having convulsions.
- Your dog has suffered a serious burn anywhere on its body.

Taking Your Dog's Temperature

Taking your dog's temperature is a little more complicated than determining some of the other symptoms. The only effective way to take a dog's temperature is by a rectal thermometer. The normal canine temperature, taken rectally, is from 100 to 102.5°F. To do this procedure correctly, first shake down the thermometer until the bulb registers 96°F. Next, lubricate the bulb with Vaseline. Raise your dog's tail while you hold the dog and tail firmly to keep the animal from sitting down. Insert the thermometer bulb gently into the dog's anus with a twisting motion, going in about one to three inches, depending on the size of the dog. Hold the thermometer in place for three minutes. Talk to your dog gently during this whole procedure to keep the animal calm. Many dogs don't mind this process at all, but some get nervous. After three minutes, remove the thermometer, wipe it clean, and read the dog's temperature by the height of the silver column of mercury on the calibrated scale. Clean the thermometer with alcohol before using it again. Please note: If the dog should sit down quickly and break the tip of the thermometer, do not attempt to find it or extract it from the dog's rectum. Instead, give one or two teaspoons of mineral oil by mouth to facilitate passage of the broken piece. Call your veterinarian.

Nonemergencies That Require Vet Intervention

Some situations are unnerving for pack parents, but they are not emergencies in themselves. Your vet should be consulted, but since it's not a matter of life and death, you can wait a day or so. These are some dog troubles that are *not* considered emergencies, though a veterinary visit is required:

- Your dog shows loss of appetite but otherwise seems well.
- Your dog has a slightly elevated temperature.
- Your dog suffers slight lameness.
- Your dog appears to be depressed but has relatively normal vital signs.
- Your dog's eyes and nose are runny.
- Your dog is coughing.

The Automobile Nightmare

If a car hits your dog, get the dog to a veterinary hospital as soon as possible. The sight of such an accident might so forcefully trigger your adrenalin that you want to rush out into traffic to save your dog. Don't do it. Stop and think first. You could be hit by oncoming traffic. If possible, ask a passerby or companion to redirect traffic so you can move the injured animal out of the street. You have to proceed quickly, but not without thinking, to get the dog off the road, especially if the vehicle that struck it has gone on and left it there. Be careful but not foolhardy. Being caught in such a predicament with a pack of dogs is a nightmare, but you must remain coolheaded and command the other dogs to stay down. If they have leashes on, you should attach them somewhere safe before trying to attend to the stricken dog. This is a tragic instance when you have to think fast and make serious decisions.

To move your dog from the road, you will probably need to improvise a stretcher, perhaps using a blanket or jacket. If a board is handy, slide the dog gently onto the board, or other makeshift stretcher and lift the stricken animal to the car, being as careful as possible not to jostle it. If you're not driving yourself and don't have a car available, try to flag one down. If this can't be done, ask someone to call a police car to assist you or do so yourself. (Please note that having a cell phone handy when out with your dogs is a wise practice.)

Don't use a tourniquet to stop bleeding if there is bleeding present. Instead, use a cloth or even your hand and apply direct pressure to the wound. If you need to improvise, you can use a bit of clothing to make a pad for absorbing blood. Don't remove it frequently because that might increase bleeding. Instead, if the blood soaks through the pad, put additional padding on top of it and keep applying pressure.

Dogs that are hit by cars do not always have external bleeding, but what's worse is that there is frequently *internal* bleeding caused by stomach or intestinal injury. The dog may cough up blood or vomit. If your dog appears okay after an automobile accident, but later on has bright red stool or a dark red-brown or black stool, go directly to the veterinarian because this is a sign of internal bleeding. After an automobile accident you should always have a vet check your dog, even if it seemed to get up and walk away unscathed.

Sometimes, dogs incur injuries that don't show up immediately. An example of this is the tumor my own dog suffered after being struck by an automobile many years ago. I had taken Grip to the veterinarian immediately. He was treated for facial and head lacerations but otherwise seemed fine, despite the freakish accident. There were no apparent internal injuries and no sign of internal bleeding. Two months later, a large tumor grew out of Grip's shoulder where it had come into the harshest contact with the vehicle that hit him. Surgery was necessary to remove the tumor; my vet traced its origin, to the best of his ability, to the trauma of impact with the car.

Shock Can Be Deadly

Dogs often go into shock after an accident. Other causes of shock are heat stroke, poisoning, hemorrhage, and severe dehydration. Shock is the condition of the body when reduced blood flow cannot properly meet the body's needs. It tries to compensate for insufficient blood flow by speeding up heart action and constricting skin blood vessels. If vital organs don't get sufficient oxygen, which is carried by blood throughout the body, the shock syndrome will continue to increase and even cause death if not treated in time.

Signs of Shock

Signs that an animal is in shock are listed below. If one or more of these conditions is present, first aid treatment must be given to alleviate shock, immediately followed up with emergency veterinary care.

- Sudden drop in body temperature
- Shivering or trembling
- Fast and weakened pulse rate, over 140 per minute
- Increased respiration, over 40 breaths a minute
- Weakness and listlessness
- Appearance of terrible mental depression
- Collapse
- Unconsciousness and/or coma

- Coldness in the animal's body, skin, and extremities
- Pupil dilation and vacant, staring eyes
- Mouth, lips, and eyelids lose color, become pale, even white

The pulse rate is the same as the heart rate, determined by counting the number of beats or pulses per minute. To take your dog's pulse, feel along the inside of the dog's thigh where its leg joins its body. The femoral artery is located there, in the animal's groin. Press your fingers until you feel the pulsation in that spot, and then count how many beats occur in one minute. Although large dogs have a somewhat slower pulse rate and smaller dogs have a faster one, for most dogs the pulse rate is about 70 to 130 beats per minute when the dog is at rest. Another place to get a pulse reading is behind the left elbow. Press your fingers there over the approximate location of the heart.

A very fast pulse indicates fever, anemia, loss of blood, dehydration, shock, infection, heat stroke, or heart and lung disease. A very slow pulse can indicate the onslaught of collapse of the circulatory system and pending fatality. It can also mean the dog has heart disease or pressure on its brain. In case of emergency, knowing how to properly take your dog's pulse is important.

Shock causes the body to lose heat quickly. Do not attempt to give the dog anything to drink if it is unconscious, having convulsions, or vomiting. If this is not the case, you can give the dog room-temperature water with glucose every half hour while awaiting veterinary care. Keep the dog's airways open by opening its mouth and wiping away any secretions. Check to see if there's a foreign body that might be preventing breathing. If so, and if you can reach it, remove it, but be extremely careful lest you push the object further into the dog's throat.

Administer artificial respiration if the dog is not breathing properly on its own. First, place the dog on its side with the right side of its body down. Apply strong force with your hands, pressing down against the chest wall. Release quickly. You can hear air moving in and out if you're doing this correctly because chest compression pushes the air out, and the elasticity of the chest draws air back in when you release the downward pressure.

This is not a difficult procedure, and you should not be afraid to try it if your dog is in such a crisis. If the compression isn't succeeding—which you will know if there's no sound of air moving in and out—you'll have to use mouth-to-nose forced respiration. First, pull the tongue forward and close the dog's mouth. Seal the dog's lips with your hand, and put your mouth over the dog's nose. Blow in steadily for three seconds. The chest will expand as you do this. Release to let the air come back out. Repeat these steps until the dog breathes on its own. Then you can start first aid treatments of wounds and take steps to alleviate shock.

To assist a dog suffering shock, wrap the dog in anything that might conserve body heat, such as a towel, blanket, or coat. Do not wrap the dog tightly, only enough to cover the dog and reduce the cooling effect of shock. Keep the dog's head lower than the rest of its body or even with the body. Massage the dog's legs and body unless the dog has a broken limb. If this is the case, the limb should be bandaged or attached to a makeshift splint until the vet can properly set it.

Throughout all of these efforts, try to keep talking gently to the dog, even if it appears unconscious. Your soothing voice can have powerful positive implications for a dog in severe distress. Stay calm to help calm down the frightened animal.

More About Transporting an Injured Dog

It's very difficult to move a large injured animal. You have to improvise a stretcher. Smaller dogs can be carried more easily. Guard and protect injured parts of the body and provide support for broken bones before you move the dog. Strap the dog onto the stretcher if possible, just as you would a person, taking care against jarring its spine, neck, or a broken limb during transport. You can't actually set the broken bones, but only stabilize them for the journey to the vet. This is very important. Keep the dog's backbone straight during transport, and try not to bend its legs. You can do this by gentle wrapping the animal in a towel, blanket, or coat in order to lift it into the vehicle.

Dogs might panic in an emergency, particularly if injured. They might bite because of fear, confusion, or pain, so guard yourself as you apply these life-saving efforts. Don't muzzle an injured dog unless it's absolutely necessary to avoid panic bites. Muzzling can interfere with breathing, so it should only be used as an absolute last resort if you cannot assist the dog without injury to yourself.

You need a very long bandage or cloth tape to muzzle a dog if you don't have a commercial muzzle. Wrap the long bandage around the dog's head, over its nose and mouth just below the eyes. Wrap it several times gently, not too tight, but sufficiently firm to prevent the dog from biting. Tie the bandage behind the dog's ears. Throughout all this, remember to keep trying to avoid jarring and sudden movements while you transport the injured animal. Pay attention to what you're doing and where you're going. If possible, call the vet ahead of time or ask someone to call the vet for you to let the emergency clinic know you're on the way with an injured dog.

Sometimes, you just have to wing it through an emergency and hope for the best. If you have a multi-dog home, you certainly want to know a little bit about these things before they happen just to be on the safe side. By reviewing this section from time to time, you can keep this information in mind and hope you'll never need it.

Wounds and Bleeding

Apply direct pressure to the bleeding wound to stop excessive flow of blood. Use sterile pads, or improvise with a torn shirt or other cloth formed into a pad and pressed down on the wound. T-shirts make good absorbent blood pads. Never use anything dirty to apply pressure to a bleeding wound. Instead of removing a soaked pad, add another layer on top of it.

If direct pressure fails to work immediately, find the nearest pressure point on the dog's body, closest to the injury, and press on it to compress the artery against the underlying bone and slow down the pumping blood from exiting the body. Use the flat part of your fingers, not your thumb or the tips of your fingers.

Don't attempt to use a tourniquet unless it is *absolutely* the last resort. Tourniquets can be dangerous and should be used in dire circumstances, for example, if the dog would bleed to death without one. Tourniquets can cause gangrene. They must be administered with extreme care. Use a one-inch-wide piece of gauze or cloth to make a tourniquet. Don't use anything so narrow that it could cut into the dog's limb. Don't use a leash. Don't use rope. If you do apply a tourniquet, release it after a short while (never more than thirty minutes), and check the flow of blood returning to the limbs before you reapply the tourniquet. Never leave a tourniquet unattended. Stay there and watch the dog carefully until the veterinarian arrives or until you get to the vet for professional medical treatment.

Blood Transfusions

Dogs have specific blood types, depending on their breed. There are eleven different blood groups. The most important canine blood type is called the A1/A2 system. Dogs that are A-negative are considered universal donors. Veterinarians in emergency-ready clinics are prepared to administer blood transfusions as needed. They cross-match to ensure compatibility between donor and recipient. If no compatible blood is available, vets will not attempt a transfusion. In life-threatening emergencies, vets have been known to use their own pets as blood donors. The number of canine blood banks in the United States is limited.

Bloat/Gastric Torsion: The Ultimate Tragedy

The word "bloat" or "torsion" strikes terror into the heart of dog lovers. Bloat and torsion have been called "the mother of all canine tragedies." Although medium dogs can also be affected, it's usually large dogs with deep chests and tucked up tummies that are more prone to this terrible tragedy. Dogs that bloat are usually around two years of age or older and mostly males. A study released by scholars at the Veterinary School at Purdue University, which specializes in the study of bloat and torsion, reported that purebred dogs are three times more likely to suffer bloat than those of mixed breed.

So, just what is this 'mother of all canine tragedies'? Bloat/gastric torsion is a life-threatening emergency whose cause is not known exactly. Bloat occurs when excessive gases are released into the stomach from fermenting food. These toxic gases cause rapid hardening and distension of the dog's stomach that usually lies in a hammock position in the abdominal cavity suspended there by ligaments at the front and rear ends. Overloaded with food, the stomach, as if it were a little hammock, swings back and forth like a pendulum going from side to side on the ligaments. As bloat continues, the stomach may flip over and pinch the ligaments at both ends, stopping the flow of blood. When blood is blocked in its normal return to the heart, shock is induced, and the stomach wall dies rapidly without sufficient blood flow. Powerful toxins are released and the dog experiences tremendous pain. It may collapse within a matter of minutes. Death often follows in as little as six or seven hours if not properly treated. Even correct and immediate veterinary care is sometimes unable to prevent death by bloat. Gastric torsion is one of the worst things that can happen to a dog.

The first part of this condition is called bloat, the swelling and distension of the stomach. Bloat doesn't always reach the second phase called gastric torsion, the twisting of the stomach on its ligaments. Sometimes, very lucky dogs *do* survive this emergency, but most often they do not. If you have the slightest suspicion of bloat occurring in your pack, take the victim to a veterinarian immediately. Do not wait. The affected dog must be X-rayed right away to see what's going on and to administer emergency treatment. How can we avoid the tragedy of bloat? Bloat prevention measures are not absolutely foolproof, but they should be strictly adhered to just the same. Follow these steps with your pack to protect your dogs as much as possible from bloat and gastric torsion:

- Never feed dogs immediately before or after heavy exercise; wait at least two hours before feeding.
- Give smaller, not larger, portions.
- Never allow dogs to drink lots of water after eating dry food.
- Moisten dry food. Do not feed only dry kibble.
- Feed the Bones And Raw Food (BARF) diet, which seems to prevent bloat.
- Don't allow dogs to gorge themselves. Limit water.

It seems that bloat is more prevalent today, not less so. Canine nutritionists strongly suspect that commercial dog foods may have a strong influence in causing it. Perhaps, too, humans live in such whirlwinds of speed and might feed their dogs inappropriately, too much, too soon. There's really no excuse for ignorance on this topic.

Symptoms That Require Immediate Veterinary Care

Dogs need *immediate veterinary attention* if one or several symptoms are present:

- Abdominal fullness or distension
- Abdominal hardness and rigidity
- Whining, crying, or pacing behavior
- Drooling, excessive salivation
- Intense panting
- Difficulty breathing
- General appearance of anxiety
- Continued frustrated efforts to vomit
- Stretching

- Gum and mucous membrane discoloration (dark red, blue, gray, white)
- Rapid heartbeat
- Weak pulse
- Collapse, coma

The last four items on the list—gum discoloration, rapid heartbeat, weak pulse and collapse—indicate severe bloat. They usually signal that death is fast approaching. You *must* get the victim to a veterinarian immediately. If your regular vet is not available, call or go directly to an emergency clinic. With the onset of second or third stage bloat (weak pulse, collapse, coma), first aid may be necessary, even on the way to the veterinarian.

There are other acute and painful abdomen emergencies in dogs that are *not* associated with bloat/gastric torsion, but have similar symptoms. They, too, are very serious health crises and require urgent veterinarian care:

- Acute pancreatitis
- Peritonitis
- Rupture of a pregnant uterus
- Rupture of the bladder
- Urinary stones
- Intestinal obstructions

fractures

Broken bones are the dramatic results from trauma. A simple fracture does not protrude through the skin, but a compound fracture breaks the skin and exposes the open wound, thereby adding the risk of infection. Bone fractures cause shock and blood loss besides being extremely painful. In such emergencies, you must treat the dog for shock as well as for the fracture.

If you think your dog has broken a bone, make a temporary splint to keep the broken limb immobilized during transport. The splint should reach beyond the break on both sides of the fracture. Wrap it around with anything that can be used as an emergency bandage, such as a necktie, segment of cloth, roller gauze if you have any handy, and so on. Nonmovement is crucial after a bone fracture, so keep the dog as still as possible, and get it to a veterinarian immediately.

Dogs and Foreign Bodies

Besides amusing us with their endless curiosity and enchantment with the world in which they live, puppies—and adult dogs, too—never tire of investigating their universe. All too frequently this results in contact with foreign bodies, sometimes of unknown origin, that mysteriously find their way into dogs' stomachs and create medical emergencies.

Foreign bodies can lead to intestinal blockages that result in life-threatening crises. Besides eating foreign objects, dogs can get serious eye and ear irritations from seeds, sawdust, dirt and insects. Scavenging dogs aren't very selective about what they ingest. Foreign objects are removed surgically or through projectile vomiting or by a painful and difficult defecation.

Dogs Eat the Darnedest Things

The following remarkable objects have come forth from dogs that ate them for some reason humans can't determine!

- Wash rags
- Nylon stockings

- Furniture stuffing
- Plastic action toys
- Batteries
- Sandwich wrappings
- String or thread
- Tin cans
- Christmas tree tinsel and ornaments

Vomiting is the first symptom you see when dogs have consumed foreign objects. They automatically attempt to evacuate nonfood items by throwing up. When dogs vomit frequently, even after drinking water, there might be intestinal blockage present.

A foreign object can remain in a dog's intestine for a long time before it is expelled. One day when my dog Grip was a youngster, I noticed how much he was straining to defecate. You can't really help a dog expel fecal matter that isn't ready to evacuate. I could see something clearly on the edge of his anus, obviously trying to come out.

Eventually, after a few more squats and groans, to my complete amazement, Grip passed a large chunk of tree bark and a small well-dented tin can! How he managed to ingest and then evacuate those two large, rough items without serious internal damage to his alimentary and digestive system is well beyond me. Fortunately, the tin can did not perforate Grip's digestive track as it made its way southward. When the offending items finally came forth, Grip looked up at me and grinned his priceless doggie smile that showed his pleasure and relief. Then, without further ado, he tore down the beach to swim in the ocean with the rest of my pack.

If you suspect any of your dogs has swallowed a foreign object that could cause an obstruction or irritation, your veterinarian will determine by X-ray or endoscopy if surgery is needed. Consult your veterinarian for foreign objects that have gotten into your dog's eyes or ears; don't try to remove them yourself. You are more likely than not to cause additional serious damage, sometimes irreversible. Take the dog to the veterinarian who has specialized tools for this emergency relief procedure.

Although dogs love to stick their heads out of car and truck windows, never allow them to do so. Foreign objects such as bugs, small pebbles, and other roadside debris can be hurled into their eyes or ears quite easily. Yes, that's right! You've got it! It's a relentless battle to prevent problems that arise in the pack from canine contact with foreign objects.

Creative Disasters

As if the foregoing didn't list sufficient nerve-wracking emergencies to deal with, some canines seem hell-bent on giving pack parents as much stress as possible. It looks like they come up with creative disasters just when you think you've got all the health and safety bases covered. Dogs in search of food or relief from boredom, when given free run of the house, often decide to sniff, chew, and swallow things that you would consider totally unthinkable, even from a dog's point of view. Nevertheless, every year veterinarians report removing such unthinkables as the television remote, for example, from the aching tummy of an unhappy canine. If you're looking around for your remote and you can't find it, check out Fido's stomach. It might sound comical, but it's not. Owners of multi-dog homes come to realize rather quickly in the life of their packs, that creative disasters seem waiting to strike. Dogs can't be trained out of kidnapping and swallowing things like the remote, so train yourself to put it away carefully out of the reach of your canine scavengers.

More About Poisoning

In Chapter 5 we included a brief discussion about poisoning. The emergency that results from poisoning bears further consideration here. In managing your multi-dog home, keep in mind that dogs find their way into all sorts of dangerous things. Casual forgetfulness on your part can lead to a terrible canine disaster.

Poison refers to any substance that can cause bodily harm. However, what is poisonous to one species is not always poisonous to another. Dogs can be poisoned from contact with toxic plants, insects, dead animals, harmful pesticides, rodenticides, cleaning materials, automobile antifreeze, and dangerous fumes. Keep all such items in locked storage where dogs have *absolutely no* access possibility. These deadly poisons kill pets. You should know the basic steps necessary to avert disaster if any of your pack might have been poisoned. Learn these emergency measures.

1. Eliminate the poison by inducing vomiting. Poisoning can sometimes be reversed by inducing vomiting. There are other circumstances in which you absolutely should *not* induce vomiting as a first aid measure for a poisoned dog. Do *not* induce vomiting if your dog:

- Is severely depressed or comatose
- Has swallowed the poison more than two hours ago
- Has swallowed a sharp object that could lodge in or perforate its esophagus or stomach

- Has swallowed a petroleum product, an acid, alkali, solvent, or heavy-duty household cleaner

If none of the above-mentioned is present, you can induce vomiting by giving your dog:

- Hydrogen peroxide at 3 percent (one to three teaspoons every ten minutes for three repetitions), or
- Syrup of ipecac (one teaspoon per 10 pounds body weight), or
- Half a teaspoonful of salt on the back of the dog's tongue

Give these to your dog in the same way as you administer any oral medication. You hold the dog's head close to your thigh with one hand while with the same hand, holding its mouth open. With the other hand pop the pill, capsule, or teaspoonful of medicine or salt onto the back of the dog's tongue. As you release the dog and allow it to close its mouth, immediately massage the throat so that the dog will swallow the medication. If the first three steps don't work, do it again, but this time, hold the dog's mouth closed while massaging the throat so it cannot spit out the medication or the salt.

2. To delay bodily absorption of poison from the dog's intestinal tract, give it mixed activated charcoal (one tablet to 10 cc water). Make the solution equal to one teaspoonful per 2 pounds body weight. Follow with a pint of water. You might have to use a stomach tube to accomplish this, so you probably need your vet to get it done correctly.

3. After thirty minutes, give the dog some sodium sulphate, one teaspoonful per 10 pounds of body weight. If you don't have sodium sulphate, give the dog Milk of Magnesia, one tea-spoonful per 5 pounds of body weight. This should cause immediate evacuation.

4. If the dog's skin has been in contact with poisonous sub-stances, wash the dog well with soap and water, lukewarm, not cold. Remove the substance that is endangering the dog lest it try to lick the affected area and swallow the poison. To remove a gasoline or oil stain from the dog's coat, soak with mineral oil or vegetable oil before washing the area with mild soap and water.

Many yard products contain arsenic trioxide or sodium arsenate for getting rid of slugs, snails, and undesirable pests. But what happens when dogs ingest these poisons? Ant elimi-nation products and weed killers are meant to kill ants and weeds, but their arsenic content might eliminate family pets as well, so be careful. Moreover, death occurs so quickly that the usual signs of thirst, drooling, vomiting, staggering, intense abdominal pain, muscle tremors, and so on, are not visible and you might not be able to get life-saving treatment in time to reverse the process. Keep these poisonous products locked away from your pack!

Dogs that ingest mouse and rat poison might suffer fatal effects that range from severe hemorrhaging to paralysis and kidney failure. Chemical burns to the esophagus result from inhaling the fumes of paint thinners and other chemicals used in yard work and deck protection. Windshield wiper fluid was reportedly responsible for the death of a dog that found it in an improperly covered container, drank some, and perished. Antifreeze smells good to dogs, tastes delicious, and kills quickly. Kidney failure is the inevitable result of drinking antifreeze, even a small amount.

Purchase the safer antifreeze that contains propylene glycol, rather than ethylene glycol. It is at least less dangerous, though that, too, should be in a proper container and *locked safely away* from pack access. Some of these poisons work so fast that permanent damage, kidney failure, and death can occur very quickly. Nevertheless, if you suspect that your dog has ingested any of these items, get it to the veterinarian immediately.

Watch out for depression, lethargy, grogginess and vomiting, the earliest symptoms. Take immediate action. There are many poison edibles that cause canine emergencies. Here are some of the better-known offenders:

• Chocolate, the number-one people pleaser, dog killer. Chocolate contains a substance known as theobromine that causes deadly heart problems in dogs. It doesn't take a lot of chocolate to create this emergency, especially in a small dog. If you know your dog ate chocolate, induce vomiting.

• Onions and garlic contain sulfides that can destroy red blood cells. Onions and garlic can be deadly for dogs.

If you think anyone in your pack has been poisoned, bring to the veterinarian any and all items that might be part of it, for example, a portion of the vomit if the dog has thrown up, the bottle or other container of poisonous household substances the dog may have ingested, or a piece of the poisonous plant. Keep the animal poison control center emergency number where you can get it easily if needed: 1-888-426-4435.

Bees, Wasps, and Other Stingers

Dogs love the great outdoors and if they could, they would spend many hours romping through fields and woods with their humans. They're great explorers, poking their noses into interesting places and what cozy corner is not? Nevertheless, lurking in the very spots they love best, such as fields, swamps, woods, caves, and so on, are mean critters that will not tolerate canine or human invasions of their territory. Bees, wasps, yellow jackets, ants, spiders, centipedes, ticks and fleas can bite and sting, giving mean and painful injuries to dogs and people alike. You and your pack don't even need to traverse very far into woods or field to make contact with these notorious monsters. They can easily find their way into your home and yard, so don't entertain false security thinking your dogs are safe from bites and stings.

Of this list, the least troublesome are ants that only bite when disturbed. Since dogs don't find them particularly tasty, they usually leave them alone. At the other end of the spectrum are the worst offenders, bees and wasps. Their stings have multiple hazardous effects. Not only do the stings of bees and wasps cause swelling and sharp pain, but they can also trigger deadly allergic reactions to the venom they deliver.

The bee's stinger pulls out of the bee's abdomen when it stings and takes the entire venom sac out with it. It empties the whole sac into its victim. Bee venom contains toxic proteins that immediately begin to attack the body systems of the victim. Dr. Steve Bentsen's article, "The Buzz on Bee Stings" (published in *AKC Afield: The Chronicle of Performance Events*), stated that, "Even if the dog escapes the allergic threat of the toxins, it still faces the toxic threat of the venom. There may be damage to the liver, kidneys, nervous system or blood cells. These effects may be seen immediately or they may not be apparent for several days. Complete destruction of the dog's red blood cells may occur despite all efforts at treatment."

If a bee stings your dog, remove the stinger with tweezers if you can get it. Do so very carefully. Wasps don't leave stingers. Make a paste of baking soda and water to apply to the affected area. Use an ice pack on the spot to relieve swelling and pain. If you're out and about in the woods or fields in the summertime, you probably carry ice water for yourself and the pack. In lieu of an ice pack, even the cold surface of a water bottle can be beneficial. Put the cold pack on for five minutes and take it off for five minutes, alternating the application over a twenty- to thirty-minute period. Soothe your dog by speaking gently and reassuringly during this painful trauma.

As a pack parent, you should be aware that while it's true that some simple stings aren't serious, if dogs are stung on the nose, mouth, around the head, or in the ears, these swellings are very bothersome. They can even cause breathing or swallowing problems. Go to your veterinarian for treatment to prevent or deflect the results of even simple stings. Multiple stings are the biggest worry.

Bees and wasps can present life-threatening dangers to your pack. A simple excursion outdoors could end up as an emergency situation, particularly if your eager-beaver pets accidentally disturb a hive or swarm. If such a disaster happens, run away from the bees or wasps as fast as you can and call your dogs with you. After the attack, get to the vet's office immediately.

Dogs must be hospitalized right away in case of massive stings. Aggressive medical treatment is needed immediately to prevent shock, maintain fluid volume, and protect inner organ systems jeopardized by the stings. Dogs that received massive stings must be closely monitored. Sometimes, they will need additional blood tests to detect damage to their inner organs. When hiking outdoors with your pack, carry an antihistamine along with you.

If your dog is stung in the mouth, bathe the area with a diluted solution of sodium bicarbonate as soon as possible. Don't linger outdoors, but return home quickly to begin treatment. Go directly to the vet if you can.

The worst insect sting I ever encountered with my pack happened to my youngest German shepherd, Abby. One summer evening, we returned home from a long hike at Floyd Bennett Field, our favorite haunt, tired and happy from our trek and having encountered nothing but delight in the day's outing. The next morning Abby's head and neck were swollen, though not a great deal. I was quite surprised since I hadn't seen a single bee, wasp, or other stinger. I was not aware that Abby had been bitten or stung. Nevertheless, I gave her two Benadryl tablets before going to work, and thank God I did! When I left the house, I had absolutely no suspicion of such a serious problem in the making. The Benadryl was simply a precaution. It might have saved her life.

Thankfully, I always remove dog collars when my pack is at home, so Abby had nothing around her neck while I was at work. If she had been collared, I am sure she would have choked to death before I returned that evening. When I got home from work, Abby's neck and head were unbelievably swollen, almost doubled in size. I rushed her to the veterinary clinic, blaming myself for not having realized hours earlier that she was in deadly danger. A single shot of antihistamine administered by the vet quickly relieved the swelling. My veterinarian explained that it was a good thing I had given Abby two Benydryl tablets that morning and removed her collar before leaving her. Keep antihistamine tablets and salve handy. You'll be glad you did.

The trouble is that dogs love to roll around on pleasant smelling lawns, and what's pleasant to the pack might be totally repulsive to us. Dogs eagerly push their noses into bushes and fragrant flowers to investigate. They like to see and smell whatever's there, and puppies are the worst offenders. They get into everything. There's no assurance other than your careful vigilance to protect the health and safety of these curious wonderful animals.

Even if you don't see an actual stinging take place, the following signs might indicate that your dog may have been stung or bitten. Get veterinary help if you notice:

- Swelling (usually face, ears or paws)
- Vomiting
- Diarrhea
- Respiratory difficulties

The last and final sign is shock and collapse (called anaphylactic shock), the precursor of death.

An interesting differentiation might be helpful. Bee stings are acid, so after removing the stinger, bathe the area in bicarbonate of soda. Wasp stings, however, are alkali, leaving no stinger in the skin. Bathe the area of a wasp sting in vinegar. In all cases, however, it's better to be safe than sorry, so contact your veterinarian immediately.

During August and September, yellow jackets get into a frenzy of territorial defense to protect their nests. They are very fierce in their competition for food and will likely crowd around picnic sites, seeking remnants of human food to eat. Attacks by yellow jackets can cause serious allergic reactions and initiate neurological symptoms.

Some spiders bite when disturbed, as do household centipedes, those multi-legged critters that sometimes appear out of nowhere and scurry madly across the floor. These can give painful bites. Centipedes, in general, however, are actually beneficial critters because they eat ants, flies, and cockroaches, the bane of apartment dwellers and sometimes pests in houses, too. Nevertheless, centipede and spider bites are painful and require a trip to the vet.

Ticks and fleas usually do not constitute emergency situations, but infestations of these pests are very troublesome. Treat your pack with one of the many excellent products available *before* ticks or fleas can attack them or make a home in their coats. In late spring and summer, ticks and fleas are at the height of their activity, so avoid their habitats, marshes, bushes, and tall grasses in woods and field, during these seasons. For locale specific pests like scorpions that abound in the southwest, consult your veterinarian and take necessary precautions as advised.

As a multi-dog owner, you might not think life-threatening emergencies could possibly arise from your dogs coming into contact with such small creatures as those discussed above. Nevertheless, it happens and that's why pack parents need to keep a good supply of anti-sting and anti-bite agents available on demand. Having these items handy will ensure against the dangers biters and stingers pose when you and your pack are trying to enjoy the great outdoors.

Bite Trauma: Breaking up Dog Fights

There are several other potential crises you should be aware of in managing your multi-dog home. If your dogs bite someone or get into a serious fight with other canines, emergency situations might result. In all my years as a dog owner and pack mother, my dogs have never bitten a person or another dog, but I've always felt responsible to be prepared to deal with just such an exigency as that should it have occurred.

You can pretty much tell if your pack are likely biters, but even if you think they're not, things can happen quite unexpectedly. If your dog bites someone, strive to remain calm, and deal with the victim gently and respectfully. Do not argue or insist that your dog is innocent. Do not accuse the victim of causing the problem whether it's the victim's own fault or not. Stay calm, cool, and collected. Be considerate of the victim and act in a kindly fashion if you have any hope at all of defusing such a potentially serious legal situation. Your behavior and attitude might be the difference between being sued or not.

Remove your dog immediately from proximity to the victim, and separate the dog from other potential victims as well. Put your dog into your vehicle if you can, or leash it to a tree or post so you can be free to assist the victim without your dog getting into additional trouble. If your whole pack is present, settle them safely away from the victim and assure the victim that as soon as the dogs are placed out of the way, you want to help and make yourself available.

Willingly and graciously give the victim your name, address, and telephone number. Tell the victim if your dog has had its regular shots and rabies vaccination. Be sincere, and not too wordy.

Help the victim obtain appropriate medical attention as needed. Offer to drive the victim to a doctor or emergency room clinic. Speak kindly and reassuringly to the victim. Get the victim's full name, address, and telephone number. Indicate your desire to be of service, not only in the present moment but also in the weeks that follow. Before you leave the scene, obtain the name, address, and telephone number of every witness. This is imperative. You must get witness information right now. Don't make any statements about the event to anyone at all because there could be criminal implications if your dog caused physical injury. Keep yourself in check against any overt emotional display. Keep in touch with the victim in the days and weeks after this event, and put forth a sincere effort to be understanding and helpful. Show yourself to be as caring about the victim's recovery as you would be about your own. These steps are essential to defuse potential legal charges against you and your animal.

Here's the catch. Your dog's *single* bite can become an enormous issue that can land you in civil court or even criminal court in the case of a serious bite or if the dog already has a bite on its record. You can be brought to dog court in which animal control authorities where you live or where the action occurred can take legal steps against you. They can even try to remove your dog, impound it, or suggest it be put to sleep. Your best bet is to absolutely avoid instigating trouble, either by talking too much or by manifesting an overly protective attitude toward your dog. Remember that in such a case, your dog is the offender. You are the dog's owner, so you stand a chance of facing serious legal proceedings against you and perhaps, even losing your pet. I can't think of too many things more horrendous than this to befall a pack parent.

Most victims will be favorably disposed toward dog and owner if the owner offers to pay the victim's medical bill, insurance deductible, or the co-payment at the doctor's office. This favorable attitude might make all the difference in the world between a victim who wants to take legal action against you and one who can forgive the dog and only wishes to get on with life.

In most places, local ordinances require reporting dog bites to the proper authorities. You *must* comply. If you don't know what's required, the Board of Health can supply the information. Call or visit the local police precinct. Your best course of action is to volunteer and not resist whatever the law requires of you as the owner of the offending dog.

Be aware that your dog might be quarantined at home with you or in an official dog pound site. Be ready to produce photocopies of your dog's most recent rabies certificate and other medical records. Give these to the victim and proper authorities as soon as possible to put the victim's mind at ease and ensure officials that everything is in proper order. This can reduce your risk of being sued.

If you think your dog has a health issue, your best bet is to volunteer to submit the animal for appropriate tests and not wait for the court to demand it. Contact your lawyer and report the incident to your insurance company to find out what other options are available to you. Be honest and open about the event. Tell the truth about your dog insofar as you are able and say exactly what happened as best you can to reconstruct the situation leading up to the bite.

However, don't make statements in advance of your lawyer's input. Untruthful statements made in haste come back to bite their owners! Wait and speak calmly with the victim, assuring him or her that you fully intend to do everything in your power to be as cooperative in resolving the issue as the victim desires you to be and has a right to expect.

While most dogs never bite people, the earlier chapters in this book provide detailed discussions of temperament and socialization requirements. If you have trained and treated your dogs properly from the beginning, including neutering or spaying animals not intended for breeding, more likely than not, you'll never have to deal with bite issues of any kind, people or dogs.

Free brochures, posters, and activity/coloring books on dog bite prevention and safety are available from the Auburn

University College of Veterinary Medicine in conjunction with State Farm. To obtain free copies, place a toll-free call to (877) 254-FIDO or visit their Web site at *www.statefarm.com.*

If your dog or another dog bites you, seek medical attention immediately. First, clean and flush the wound with clear water. Ask the owner of the other dog for his or her name, that of the offending animal, address, and telephone number. Give yours willingly if requested.

Fighting Furries

Dog squabbles are normal events, whether at home in the pack or elsewhere in play areas where dogs run free. These don't usually lead to serious fights. Dogs can get agitated and start to be rough and tough trying to establish dominance. They may even engage in serious aggressive behavior. Some dogs become prejudiced against others or hold grudges from past experiences. If you haven't had the foresight to separate your dogs when a fight was brewing or to remove them from free-roaming dogs not of your pack, think about what you must do to break up the fight once it breaks out. Here are a few pointers:

- Scream loudly at the canine fighters.
- Throw water on the embattled dogs. Use a garden hose if one is handy.
- If possible, pick up a large object, a piece of branch or a shovel and hold it at arm's length to protect yourself as you charge into the dogfight, yelling loudly and pushing the dogs aside from one another with the object you're holding. (This takes some courage.)
- Grab a coat, blanket, or towel and cover or wrap it

quickly around the heads of the dogs, blocking their vision to confuse them into momentary separation.

- Grab hold of the closest dog's tail or rear legs and drag it out of the fight and away from the other dogs. It's best, of course, if you can then confine that fighter before you go back to drag off another one.
- Do *not* spray with chemicals that can cause irreparable damage to dogs, such as ammonia, pepper mace, and so on.

Examine your dogs after any kind of an aggressive encounter with other canines. Check for serious bites that may need veterinary attention.

Hot Weather Blues: Heat Stroke and Exhaustion

Even the weather can precipitate pack emergencies. Dogs are easy prey to heat stroke, a condition that makes them appear groggy or renders them unconscious. Confinement in poorly ventilated crates, kennels, or cars can cause heat stroke. Dogs become frantic, feeling trapped, while their body temperatures rise and they are unable to get relief. Their frantic activity only increases their body heat and brings on exhaustion and coma. It doesn't take long for a dog to die in overheated conditions. Heart failure and brain damage can also be caused in a very short period of time by overheating.

If your dog is on the verge of heat stroke or is suffering from exhaustion, take it to the nearest animal hospital for emergency veterinary care. Don't wait. When traveling in hot weather, even on short local trips, always bring plenty of cool water with you. Wet down its body and paws with cool water, and fan the dog with any kind of makeshift arrangement to move air into its face. Contrary to popular belief, dogs can suffer heat stroke in their own homes when not properly ventilated. Dogs that overexert during exercise or play can develop the same physical conditions as when confined to an overheated environment. The symptoms of heat stroke or overexertion are the following:

- Panting
- Slobbering
- Vomiting
- Diarrhea
- Raised body temperature

When dogs suffer heat stroke or overexertion, they can quickly collapse and become comatose, eventually dying if not relieved. To rescue a dog from heat stroke or overexertion, remove it immediately from the hot place and take it into a cool or shady area. Soak the dog with cold water from a hose or cold bath if possible. As you do so, or immediately thereafter, massage the dog gently to stimulate blood circulation as the temperature slowly returns to normal. Give the dog a little water to drink as soon as it becomes conscious. While it is still unconscious, you can wet its lips and mouth area with a sponge or cloth, but do *not* pour water into the dog's throat or attempt to make it drink until it revives sufficiently.

Dogs in heat prostration or heat stroke might require artificial respiration (described in Chapter 13) before they can breathe adequately on their own. Never permit your pack to exercise vigorously in extreme temperatures. Dogs don't sweat. They pant for heat relief. Be alert, and take action before your dog begins to pant excessively. Stop its activity. Remove the dog to a cooler environment immediately. Wet the dog down right away as explained above. Avoid traveling when it's too hot. Unexpected travel delays when it's extremely hot outdoors can pose increased risks to pets in cargo during air travel, but this is also the case in automobiles, so be sure your car air conditioning works properly if you plan to drive with your pack during extreme heat.

Hypothermia and Frostbite

Hardy breeds enjoy outdoor fun in frigid weather, but prolonged exposure to cold causes body heat to plummet, especially if canine coats get soaked through. Dogs suffer hypothermia (abnormal low temperature) when their internal temperatures drop below 96°F. Small dogs and those with short hair or clipped coats more rapidly succumb to hypothermia from prolonged chilling. Small dogs should wear protective sweaters when out in extreme cold weather. Dogs that begin to shiver should be taken indoors immediately and not remain in the cold.

Body energy burns up rapidly and dissipates when external temperatures or wind chills drop below freezing and blood sugar levels sink. Dogs become listless and violent shivering is followed by apathy as they slip into unconsciousness from overexposure.

Do not expose your pack to extreme cold. To treat dogs for hypothermia, first wrap them up in a blanket, coat, or other warming material. Remove them from the cold as soon as possible. Give warm baths to alleviate severe cold endured by wet dogs in icy weather. Towel the dogs off rubbing vigorously to dry the fur and skin and to encourage circulation. Apply warm water packs (about 105°F, similar to the temperature of a baby's bottle prepared for feeding) to chest and underbelly. You want to bring body temperature up to at least 100°F, so continue warm packing or using a hair dryer gently to warm the dog. Give honey-water or sugar-water at lukewarm temperature as the dog begins to revive and is able to swallow without choking.

In the case of frostbite, gently warm affected areas by soaking with warm water for brief periods of about fifteen minutes each. Do not rub too roughly with a drying towel because the skin will be irritated from the frostbite. It might be necessary to administer an antibiotic ointment and wrap the injured area with a bandage to prevent or treat frostbite induced infection that can be very painful to the dog. Seek veterinary care immediately.

Besides frostbite, there is something else that can cause emergency distress in your pack during cold weather. Ice-melting chemicals and salt put on sidewalks in the wintertime can brutally burn canine footpads. Avoid surfaces that have been treated with salt or ice-melting chemicals. Wash your pack's footpads with warm water immediately upon returning indoors. Pads can become very painful from salt and chemical burns.

Burns and Electric Shock

Dogs are susceptible to heat burns, chemical burns, and electric shock. The first is heat burns, the most commonly suffered. Like most animals, dogs fear fire. Reluctant to approach an open flame, dogs do not sustain burns of this type. Dogs might burn their pads walking on hot asphalt. Dogs have been scalded by accidents involving hot water. For heat burns like these, treat as follows:

- Apply a clean cloth soaked in cold water, and hold it to the burned area.

- Never use grease or butter or an ointment on such a burn.
- Cover the burn with a wet dressing. Wrap the body part in thick dry towels until you can get the dog to a veterinarian. Keep the dog lying down quietly.
- Give the dog fluids if dehydration is suspected and the animal is not vomiting.
- Treat the dog for shock if necessary.

The second type is a chemical burn. Wash the burned area with plenty of clean, fresh water. If the burn is from acid, use a solution composed of one-teaspoon bicarbonate of soda to one liter of water. Apply freely. If it's an alkali burn, the plain water wash suffices. After the chemical burn has been well washed, apply a soothing ointment, either a commercial product or olive oil.

Closely related to burns are electric shock emergencies where a dog has chewed through wires or cables. These can cause a dog to go into shock, but not always. In some dogs, reaction to electrocution comes several hours after the fact, not immediately. So, if you suspect your dog has had contact with electricity, go to the veterinarian immediately. Don't wait for the delayed reaction.

Protecting the Pack in a Natural Disaster or Large-Scale Civic Emergency

Since September 11, we've all become much more aware of the possibilities of disaster striking out of the blue, totally without warning. Natural disasters and human-caused large-scale civic emergencies are difficult enough in their own right, but if you have a pack of animals stranded somewhere unreachable, such events are an absolute nightmare. The only thing you can do about natural disasters or large-scale civic emergencies is to try planning in advance a basic plan of action to ensure the protection of your pets.

Be prepared to evacuate the pack as safely and smoothly as possible from a threatened area if there is sufficient warning that a disaster is pending. You need a plan in advance of where and with whom you might place the pack for shelter, keeping in mind that many human disaster shelters simply refuse to permit residents to include their pets with family members. It would be an agonizing decision for most multi-dog owners to figure out what to do in that alternative. I could never just leave my dogs and cats in the face of danger to fend for themselves. The only other alternative is to come up with some way to accommodate them should the unthinkable happen.

First, try to line up a few alternative persons or places where your pack will be safe, with you, or in your absence if you are detained elsewhere. Give one or several responsible and similarly dedicated individuals the keys to your home for the purpose of evacuating pets if something disastrous happens. Agree ahead of time what to do for them until you can return. Each situation will be different, but all disaster emergencies are horrendous to consider. Perhaps you could be instrumental in planning with other animal owners close to where you live how best to rescue each other's animals in such emergencies if no mass shelter for pets has already been set up. Check for what may be available near you and if nothing is, start the ball rolling yourself.

For an emergency exit from your home and the possibility of emergency shelter occupancy, pack in advance an emergency bag including your own medical insurance papers and your pack's health records and veterinary certificates of vaccination to assure shelter keepers and other guests that your pets don't pose any threat of communicable diseases to complicate the disaster already in progress. Shelters might even require proof of vaccinations and refuse animals not accounted for with the proper records. We would hope no pet would be denied access for that reason, but don't take anything for granted.

If you don't have a vehicle, ask someone who drives about the possibility of driving you with your pets to an appointed place of safety should emergency warnings be issued. Keep your emergency bag ready to go. Along with health and vaccination records, include emergency food for the pack and a few favorite toys. Stick in an old shirt or trousers of yours to comfort the dogs.

An emergency temporary caretaker should be authorized by you in advance to make decisions necessary for the well-being of your pack. That could also include the decision to euthanize if something occurred that made life support impossible and demanded mercy for the injured or sick animal. Before completing arrangements between you, instruct your caretaker fully about everything that might be needed. Keep a good stash of food, treats, and canine medications on hand so no emergency catches you up short. If you plan to vacate your pets to a specified haven, such as a private home, keep another stash there as well.

My neighbor's death occurred recently and was not discovered for several days, during which time her three cats were left alone, unfed, and unattended. If these had been dogs, it would have been even more tragic because dogs need more human care than cats. Prepare for personal emergencies as well as national disasters or civic unrest before such things happen. The pack totally depends on you. Thinking ahead is the best thing you can do to ensure their protection.

The Emergency Pack

A few pointers worth keeping in mind planning for the pack, should you suffer a personal emergency, are these:

- Keep your wallet card current with the proper emergency contact names and telephone numbers.
- Have a leash and collar for each dog in a place near the door that is easily accessible. Tell your back-up people where it is.
- Keep pet vaccinations up to date and accounted for in your emergency bag.
- Place a "Pets Inside" rescue sticker on the door of your apartment or home and on the windows so emergency rescuers will know there are animals inside.
- Exchange personal phone numbers, cell phone numbers, veterinary clinic numbers, and home keys with your pack protection partner for emergencies.

After doing everything you can to ensure your pack's well-being in advance of national disasters or personal emergencies, the best you can do is hope and pray they never happen. On the positive side, it is interesting and uplifting to know that many pets reportedly have survived all kinds of disasters and managed to live long happy lives afterwards. Animals are a great personal responsibility and a terrific added worry during times of crisis, but they are also the most constant and uncompromising comfort in the world.

In the aftermath of September 11, many individuals described how their pets came to the fore with their unimaginable unconditional love and gave the suffering people a shoulder to cry on night and day as needed. I know my own pack provided me with many hours of comfort. They seemed to sense the trauma and angst of September 11 that countless New Yorkers experienced, I among them. Many dogs proved themselves heroes that day and in the months that followed.

Dog Pack Parents' First Aid Kit

Having a first aid kit is not only a good idea for your multi-dog home, but significant and imperative. Keep one in the car and one at home. When you travel, take it along. You can put together your own canine first aid kit or purchase one prepackaged commercially. Either way, here's a list of essential items to include:

- Hydrogen peroxide
- Buffered aspirin (Dogs should not be given Tylenol, but aspirin is fine for them.)
- Eyewash
- Antibiotic ointment (preferably triple)
- Rubbing alcohol
- Hydrocortisone acetate (1 percent cream)
- Pepto Bismol tablets
- Immodium, Kaopectate, or other antidiarrhea medication
- Benadryl capsules (25 mg, for allergies)
- Ace self-adhering athletic bandage (3-inch width)
- Sterile, nonadherent pads
- Gauze sponges
- Sterile stretch gauze bandage (3 inches by 4 yards)
- Bandage scissors
- Vet Rap bandage
- Custom splints
- Ear syringe (two ounce capacity)

- White petroleum jelly (Vaseline or similar)
- Dermicil hypoallergenic cloth tape (1 inch by 10 yards)

Preparedness can make all the difference, so think about each item as you add or subtract at will. Commercially prepared Dog First Aid kits are available from *www.mickiesplace.com* and also at *www.sitstay.com*.

Important Information to Keep Handy

Make yourself a list of emergency numbers, and keep it posted where it will be readily available in a necessity. The best resource for an animal poison emergency is the ASPCA Animal Poison Control Center, available round the clock every day of the year. This number should be first on your list at home and in your wallet!

Have these names and telephone numbers at the ready:

- 1-888-426-4435 (National Animal Poison Control Center)
- 1-800-984-8638 (National Pet Recovery Hotline)
- 1-800-555-6517 (Animal Legal Defense Fund)
- 1-800-227-4645 (Emergency Disaster Hotline provided by the American Humane Society)
- 1-888-478-7574 (Pet Loss Support Hotline)
- Your local veterinarian
- Another vet or emergency clinic
- Contact persons who could help in an animal emergency
- An all-night animal emergency hotline in your area (for this information, check with the local ASPCA)
- Several animal shelters near you with address and telephone numbers of each

It's impossible to keep on top of every possible kind of emergency dogs might encounter over a lifetime, especially if you have a pack, but knowing the essential steps to administer first aid properly until veterinary care can be obtained is singularly important in a multi-dog home. Even if you can't learn everything you'd like to know about emergency care of the pack, having at least a rudimentary knowledge of these things could save the lives of one or more of your dogs. I strongly urge you to read a couple of books on the topic of canine emergencies and keep them in your home library.

Principles for Dealing with Canine Crises

Several principles should be uppermost in your mind when dealing with canine crises. The first rule of thumb is to *think clearly and stay cool*. The second is to address pack fears during an emergency by soothing them in a gentle voice as you carry out the practical steps necessary while awaiting veterinary intervention. The third thing is to remember that no one is infallible and accidents happen, so don't blame yourself. Finally, ground yourself in reality. Become a centered, focused individual if you're not one yet. Accept life as it is, so when it throws you a curve, you can meet the challenge without falling apart. After all, that's exactly what dogs do. They are so resilient. Whatever happens, you and your pack will be better off in the long run if you take the time to be prepared. Readiness is empowerment in the face of any emergency. When you feel ready, you can handle crises with equanimity and courage.

If I have any beliefs about immortality,
it is that certain dogs I have known will go to heaven,
and very, very few persons.
—James Thurber

Chapter 13

A Terrible Mercy: When You Must Put Your Canine Friend to Sleep

In as much as ownership connotes the possession of a thing, or the eradication of an individual personality, I am not a dog owner, no. Much rather, to the extent that our relationship is characterized by humor, loyal companion-ship, spirit, and grace, my dog(s) and I are grateful friends and partners.

—Klinger Laubscher

E verything that comes into our lives will leave us one day for nothing is permanent and no one is exempt from parting. Separation awaits all of us. We must all experience the heart-wrenching loss of those we love that love us, too. With all other living things, we are caught up in the ebb and flow of time, our existence sewn with measured moments that finally go down to death. My father's words of wisdom have been my lifelong guide: "Everything that lives must die," and loss is a journey every heart must make. The path of parting leads through tunnels of darkness, longing, and grief, until, gradually, with great effort, we can turn again toward wholeness, reviving ourselves in hope as we process the memory of who and what it was that took leave of us making such a void in the universe. It's a terrible mercy pack parents and other animal lovers must endure when, for the sake of a higher good, they must put their canine friends to sleep.

Dogs come into our lives for just a little while. We gather them joyfully into our hearts and welcome them into the pack as they take their places in the canine units that live intimately with our human families. Dogs are our best companions and dearest friends, citizens of another species, dwelling in the deepest intimacy of our homes, knowing our secrets, sharing our joys and sorrows, wrapping us in unconditional love to keep us safe, secure and strong in their irrevocable friendship. Dogs give us the kind of loyalty that never fails, devotion we can always trust, comradeship unselfish and without pretense. No matter what is going on around us or within us, our dogs are there to see us through. They are fair-minded players in the world, good sports in the game of life. They find our humor to their liking and give us pause to smile and laugh despite the challenges we face.

Dogs make play an act of worship. Their every movement is choreography of love as they dance the dance of our making, its rhythms set by us. They enchant us with their charm and good nature, taking us just the way we are and finding us quite wonderful, thank you, gods and goddesses in their sight. To love a dog is one of life's most special gifts. To love several is happiness not possible for many people, yet enviable to all. In your multi-dog home, you need not fear the darkness of the night or the loneliness of dawn. Your dogs are watchful. They are there, and all will be well.

Parting from the dogs we love is never easy. The canine lifespan is somewhere between six and ten normally, sometimes more than ten, and miraculously, occasionally even fourteen or fifteen years, a short time on this planet for such wonderful creatures.

It is not morbid to realize that the puppy licking your face this very moment will accompany you as a devoted sidekick for a very limited number of years before you must surrender it back to its creator and accept the pain of parting. That's just the way it is. No one is exempt. No one gets away without saying goodbye. Nevertheless, in the final analysis, to live with dogs and to let them go when the time comes is like everything else in life, something more to learn, an opportunity to grow, another nudge pushing us to wake up to reality and seek our true happiness in enlightenment, the ability to accept life as it is and let go.

The Most Difficult Decision in Your Dog's Life

It's all been a series of decisions right from the very beginning. Taking this dog into our lives, cherishing it—a big decision. Creating the pack and making choices of how we shall live together and love each other, human and canine family members, bring us eventually to the final, last decision and most difficult of all. You take stock now, remembering each choice you made along the way. Shall you get a dog? Shall you get a male or female, young or mature animal, purebred or mixed, from a breeder or shelter? Shall you have one dog or several? Shall you neuter, spay or not? Shall you feed this brand or that, and now, finally, the final decision, the ultimate: shall you put your pet to sleep? How can you abide this last terrible mercy?

Faced with this awesome question, we must gather our deepest inner resources to make a decision based solely on what is best for the dog, not what *we* want, not what *we* feel, but what is *best and kindest for the dog*. That is the only criterion for justice and love to prevail in the final, most difficult decision of pack life. I had a dog with heart disease and cancer. I had to let him go. I had another with severe crippling hip dysplasia. I had to let her go. I had a third with kidney failure. I had to let him go. I had a fourth with cardiogenic shock after an accident. I had to let her go. Four times in too few years, great dogs made their exits from my life and facing each loss, each parting, was all over again, a terrible lesson in the acceptance of reality, such as it is, not as I want it to be.

The Steps to Euthanasia

The decision to euthanize follows a series of inevitable steps. Although you may know them well, let's take a moment to consider the realities that lead to putting a dog down as the last and kindest mercy, a terrible one at that. We must make the ultimate decision for the benefit of every dog we have unless nature takes its course and mercifully ends the dog's life before we must do so.

- A life threatening or terminal illness is diagnosed.
- The prognosis is poor and medical care, extremely expensive and difficult to afford, cannot do anything but only delay the inevitable.
- Necessary veterinary care would require many extra visits to the veterinary clinic and a difficult medication regimen that would be hard on the dog and owner.
- Other treatment options are likewise staggering to consider.
- The dog is suffering, losing appetite, becoming weaker, and gradually the life force is breaking down.
- A sense of overpowering sadness and the burden of decision rests heavy on your heart.
- You wait and hope that things will get better, but they don't.
- Friends and family suggest putting the dog to sleep.
- Other pack members are obviously concerned and disturbed by the condition of the ill pet.
- You wait a little longer and then you blame yourself later for waiting too long, perhaps allowing the beloved pet to suffer more than necessary.
- You rejoice when your pet has a few good days and you think perhaps the tide is turning, but then you know it's only a momentary reprieve.
- You struggle more with your decision.
- You try to cope with its reality.

- Your pet continues to fail, but never takes its eyes off of yours.
- You speak much with the animal and caress it tenderly.
- You know what you must do and so does the sick dog. The other animals are sad and tentative.
- You make arrangements with your veterinarian to carry out your decision.
- Your beloved pet is pampered and loved even more than ever before, but you know for sure that nothing more can be done. It's time.
- You let pack members spend some time with the sick dog.
- You watch them carefully, sensing that they know something very serious is happening.
- You talk to them and to the sick animal, explaining, comforting, sharing your grief, and trying to be brave for their sake.
- If you have children, you go through the same process, loving, talking, gently preparing them to say goodbye to the beloved dog.
- You don't know how much dogs can understand, but somehow you realize they seem to grasp it all, both pack members and the dying dog.
- You take your beloved pet on its last journey to the veterinary clinic where, mercifully, it will be put to sleep without pain, and gently returned to its maker.
- You hold the animal in your arms and speak to it softly while the work of termination is compassionately carried out, easing the dog into eternity.
- The dog looks at you for the last time, its eyes focused and then losing focus, as it stares into your eyes and says its silent goodbye, vision blurring, heart slowing.

- In seconds, it is all over, and your pet is gone.
- Now you put your loving arms around the lifeless body of your old pal and even though you know you made the right decision, there is a howling loss rising up within you and then grief like a rock is lodged in your heart.
- Oh, how much it hurts, this terrible mercy, this ultimate act of love, choosing your pet's last moment, this kindness removing it from suffering and pain, this difficult final agonizing choice.
- Now, there is cremation or burial, and you say your last farewell.

It is unthinkable to prolong the life of a suffering animal just because we cannot bear the pain of separation. Yet well-meaning people do just that all the time. I don't know why. I cannot see the love or wisdom in keeping dogs alive when they cannot stand, can barely eat, are nearly blind, fumbling and falling with balance gone, and so deteriorated that life has no quality, but only a starkness waiting for the end. Is this the quality of mercy that dogs deserve? Do they not deserve the dignity of a last farewell in your arms, surrounded by love, with mercy and gentleness, rather than prolonged sickness and insupportable suffering? I know some otherwise wonderful dog people who just cannot face the decision to euthanize a beloved dog. I believe it is morally wrong for us to let a dog's life drag on painfully when accepted and justified veterinary practice could abbreviate its suffering.

The decision to let dogs go is horrendously difficult, almost as terrible as pulling the plug on a life support system that does nothing more for the patient than mechanically keep the body pumping blood and processing oxygen after the brain is completely without light. But these are facts of life. It seems to me the greater part of love and loyalty should enable us to put aside our monstrous grief and do what is best for the pet, no matter how hard for us. Children must be helped during this process so that they can gently come to acceptance. Their ability to understand what is happening is limited the younger they are, but as the pack parent, you must make every effort before, during, and after the loss of pets to sustain and assist children in the family with the reality of terminating animal life. Allowing children and other family members to take part in the discussion preceding this weighty decision, giving all of them the facts and helping them to understand that what is about to happen, is not cruel or mean-hearted, but an act of loving mercy. For a beloved animal, you will afford closure its rightful opportunity for everyone concerned.

Children might want to be present when their pet is put to sleep. If the child is capable of going through this experience, and if you are capable of providing support and comfort, it's not a bad idea at all to permit a child this opportunity to share the dog's final moment and say his or her last goodbye. In a very real way, this tragic moment might be key to helping the child make friends with death, an inevitable player in the game of life.

No one can make the final decision for you. As pack leader, you are alpha, and only alpha has the right and responsibility to choose. Your choice must be based on reaching for the highest good of all, the sick or aged pack member, other members of the pack, yourself, and your human family.

For me, the only choice that made sense in each instance was to terminate the suffering my dogs would have continued to endure had I not let them go mercifully free into the timeless, eternal beyond from which they were created. It was never easy. Heartbreaking and soul-wrenching, it was still my duty, only mine, completely mine, a terrible mercy indeed.

My dogs would die for me. This I have known about each and every one of them, and about all of them together as my pack. To protect me they would fight to the death if it were ever necessary and with their last ounce of strength, they would go down to death courageously on my behalf, these, my loyal, faithful, best and dearest friends. I could do no less for them, for each one individually and for them all as a pack. It was only possible for me to make these decisions about euthanasia in the light of the reflections I have shared here. My dogs lived wonderful, happy lives, and I could not condemn them to certain endless, debilitating pain and suffering.

Whatever lies beyond death, nothing or something, glorious or not, death itself is the great leveler before which everything is equal and nothing is superior. We with our dogs, great and small, stand on level ground in the face of death, equal with all other living beings that must also die. In that formidable moment, the common history of our lives, all our thoughts, words, and deeds, all our dreams on this planet and beyond come to silence at the end. Death has no favorites.

Two options

There are two options from which you can select the most compassionate way to handle the euthanasia of your dog. The first is having the vet come to your home to put the animal to sleep. If you choose this option, you may do so in the presence of the other pets because animals deal with grief in a natural way. The sight and smell of the deceased makes it easier for pack members than when a dog is removed from the home and never returns. The dying pet is much more comfortable in its own environment, too, letting go of its life among familiar sounds and smells, a sense of home and family comforting it as much as any dying creature can be comforted.

The second option would be to take your pet to the vet's office for euthanasia. At the veterinarian's place, your animal will probably be taken with you into a quiet room and you will be able to stand beside the examination table while it is tranquilized. If the vet doesn't invite you to be present at the termination of your dog, request this. Do not accept a negative reply. Talk to your dog the whole time and even during the final moments of the process, for hearing is the last thing to go. Repeat how much you love the dog and what a wonderful friend it has been to you. If the other dogs are around, allow them to sniff the empty shell that remains after the dog's death. Dogs do understand that their pack buddy is no longer there in the empty shell that lies before them. In the wild, pack members would sniff and circle, circle and sniff. Then they would leave the deceased packmate and go forth without it. It is life that must prevail and nature equips the pack to go on living. Were we ourselves deeply immersed in the reality of the universe, we, too, would go on living after the loss of a beloved friend, lover, parent or child. Even here, they teach us, our wonderful dogs and dearest friends, true angels in fur coats with four legs and a tail. Theirs is always a mission of mercy to us.

Disposition of Your Pet's Remains

Deciding on the best disposition of animal remains after death is part of the process and there are several options you should consider. You can leave the deceased with your veterinarian and allow the vet to make the final disposition, which would ordinarily be to cremate your dog in a group cremation. To obtain your dog's ashes after cremation, make your request known to the vet ahead of time so that arrangements can be made to cremate your dog by itself and return the ashes to you.

Some pack owners choose to bury the departed dog near their homes in the backyard or some other suitable place. A friend of mine plants roses above each of her dogs' graves. When she moves from her current residence, she plans to excavate all the graves, cremate any remains that are still visible, and take the dust of her beloved dogs with her to the new location wherever it might be. There are beautiful pet cemeteries in most major cities and in small towns, too. You can have your dog interred and put a grave marker of your selection to name the spot uniquely your pet's lasting resting place. Then you can return there as often as you wish.

A friend of mine lost his two beloved German shepherd dogs to old age and illness in sequence of each other during a short period of one year. When he adopted a young German shepherd male at the local shelter many months later, the first thing he did was to take the adoptee to visit the pet cemetery where the beloved departed shepherds are buried. To his lasting amazement and comfort, the new dog, only ten months old and without any prior contact, went directly to the correct grave site and stood silently over the graves of his forerunners. The man and his wife visit the site so often that maybe it was the master's scent that lingered there, and the new dog might have been familiar with it from riding in the man's vehicle. Although the old dogs were buried many months earlier, it is also possible that their remains were not yet fully decomposed, so, perhaps their scent lingered. Whatever it was, my friends were deeply moved. They declared that Max, their new German shepherd son, had found his rightful family!

A third dog owner whom I have known for many years left the remains of her most cherished dog on the beach at Coney Island. As a naturalist, she reasoned that the body of her beloved little terrier should be given over to nature and returned to the earth. She did not think it amiss that her pet's body might be pulled out to sea by the tide or even eaten by feral animals on the beach. At first, this seemed to me an awful choice for the disposition of an animal, but as I reflected further, I came to see the wisdom in letting nature take its course. The section of beach where her dog was left to rest, is far removed from the traffic of Coney Island, and in that desolate piece of shore so seemingly distant from the busy world of the city, his little body was quickly taken back into the earth and sea. As scripture says, "Remember man, that thou art dust and unto dust thou shalt return." My friend has no trouble with her decision to lay the dog she loved best on the very beach where he often played and cavorted.

I buried one of my pack members in a distant woodland area just outside the city. The grave was dug as deep as I could manage and there I left my precious bundle, wrapped in an old T-shirt of mine, laid to rest underneath the earth at the foot of a beautiful tree. To this day although several years have passed, my dog Abby goes immediately and directly to the spot and stands silently near the grave whenever we return to those woods.

It's up to you how to dispose of your beloved dog's remains, but do not allow this responsibility to add to your grief. Rather, let it be a choice and action that gives you peace and closure. Do what you feel most comfortable doing and nothing else. In the final analysis, whether family or friends agree with how you dispose of your pet's remains, it's your choice after all. You are the one who has cared for this creature during life and you are the one most affected by its death. Your pack was enlivened by its presence and is diminished by its death.

Whatever you decide to do with the body of your departed

dog, do it with the conviction that everything that lives must die and all beings in the end must surrender their material bodies back into nature. Burial, cremation, or abandonment to the elements are different in mode only. Essentially, they are the same, the last farewell and final ministry for those we love. Every culture in the world has its own way of parting with beloved ones. As long as you do not violate any health requirements of the area in which you choose to dispose of your dog, let your conscience be your guide.

Dealing with Grief

Dealing with the loss of a beloved pet requires a strong commitment to life and to those members of the pack that survive. Together, you and your pack will regroup and life will go on. In the next section, I will talk about helping the other pack members deal with their grief, but right now, what about yours? The dogs in our lives are such beloved friends and family members, that our grief at their demise is a normal, natural experience, intense though it may be. More than anything else, dogs are a constant and reliable presence so their absence tugs at our heartstrings long after they are gone. The routines dogs made necessary for us give a certain structure and balance to the way we live and because of them, we have hopefully become a little less selfish and more altruistic. By continuing to reach out to the pack and to other people during our own grieving process, our hearts will be healed more quickly and we will be able to move on that much sooner. Dogs provide us with unconditional love seldom found anywhere else. If your heart is broken when your dog is gone, don't blame yourself for feelings of desolation and despondency, depression and devastation.

Don't be surprised that some family members and friends might not be able to understand the depth of your pain. Others should never dictate how you should feel or what you should feel or what you need to do about it. This is your loss, your pain because this was your dog. It's truly wonderful when people close to us provide support and comfort during the seasons of our grief, but don't blame them if they can't. For you and me, perhaps, a dog is not 'just a dog' but a special being irreplaceable in the universe. Others don't always feel that way, even if they liked the particular pet now deceased. Nevertheless, many people *do* understand what you're going through and many of them have already gone through it themselves, perhaps not once, but several times. Others that also love their pets, know all too well that it's your grief today and tomorrow it will be theirs for this is the inevitable cycle of life.

Grief is often intertwined with other negative feelings like guilt, anger, denial, hurt, alienation, despondency, and depression. They can be a formidable burden, so be patient and gentle with yourself. Eventually, when the time is right, you'll consider giving a spot in your heart and in your home to another dog, another puppy or oldster, another being to love, a new furry someone to be welcomed into the precincts of your pack. You can never replace the one that's gone, but don't let that prevent you from taking another dog and don't feel disloyal for loving it deeply. The new dog will be an individual, unique and different, not a replacement at all, but a new entity altogether.

So let your heart speak to you, and let your head decide, but take your time and don't be pressured. Life will *not* be the same as it was; that's a fact. Life is never the same. It's a flowing river of time that you can't step into twice in the same place. But life goes on and as it does, we learn to live and laugh again, no matter how deep or agonizing our loss has been.

Bereavement counseling can help if you are grieving the death of a beloved pet. If you don't know where to turn for someone to talk with, ask around and don't be ashamed to acknowledge your feelings of sadness and loss. Face up to the real needs your dog's death might have created in you. This is not at all a sign of weakness or cowardice. It is instead a sign of your deep love for the furry kid who shared your life for all those years. Nothing can be more honorable and understandable. Be patient with yourself and with your pack because they, too, are grieving, as we shall see later.

Physical exercise and activity can help you move through the grieving process. If you focus on getting back into action with the remaining members of the pack, you'll find yourself feeling better each day. Seclusion and sedation are not the answer to grief. They only exacerbate its debilitating effects. But when we grieve, probably the last thing we want to do is physical exercise, with or without our other dogs. Mistake. Take another look. They need it and so do you. Strive manfully to get past the initial feelings of inertia that accompany grief and follow the path to healing.

Helping Children Through the Bereavement Process

If you're a parent with youngsters of any age who also loved the dog, give each child the opportunity, not once but as often as possible, to talk about his or her feelings. Never suggest to a child or adult in the face of grief that he or she should "be strong" and not succumb to tears and sorrow. That's ridiculous. The best way to pass through the valley of darkness and loss is to be real about it. Being real means accepting and expressing what we feel, talking about it and sharing it, working through and finally being healed. That's why grief is called a process. This can be a time of spiritual searching, too, so don't be afraid to ask the hard questions that are in your mind. Talk about your feelings. Prayers of thanksgiving offered during grief not only give expression of our appreciation and gratitude for having shared life with a beloved dog, they also lift the heart and mind beyond this earthly paradise to the one that never fails.

When trying to help youngsters deal with grief at the loss of a pet, be as positive as possible, but also be completely honest and realistic. Use the terminology of truth. Don't try to make nice. Don't attempt to cover over the pain of death by speaking to children in euphemisms that convey a sugarcoated falsity unworthy of the child's dignity. Even very young children can grasp the idea of death, dying, loss, separation and grief. They know the feelings they experience. It's up to us as parents, relatives, and friends to give children the correct information and to be there for them as they work through their emotional response.

It's a big mistake to suggest to children that a dead pet is not dead but has merely left the household or run away or been given to someone else. This falsehood creates additional problems as the child's mind tries to figure out why a beloved pet has abandoned him or her. If your pet was euthanized, tell your child the truth. Explain how difficult it was to make the decision to put a beloved dog to sleep, but that love made you do it in order to prevent further suffering. Explain to the child that the dog was not going to get better and it was kinder and more loving to stop its pain than to let it continue. Encourage the child to express what he or she feels as you tell the truth about a pet's death. Pause and let the child speak or just be silent together. Let the child cry if he or she seems to want that release. Be patient, loving, and take your time. Dealing with death and loss is a very important developmental step in a youngster's life.

Don't be ashamed or embarrassed to show your true feelings about the dog's death. Children do best when adults are *explicitly real* in dealing with grief and loss. They are enabled to feel whatever emotions arise within them without trying to hide the reality of their pain and grief.

One grief counselor suggested that kids be involved in some project to memorialize the deceased dog, for example, planting something in memory of the pet. Encourage your child to draw or write about the deceased pet, perhaps to make up a poem in its memory. These creative efforts give youngsters an opportunity to express themselves in other ways besides crying and depression. There are memorial sites on the Internet that provide places for people to share photos of their beloved deceased pets online along with dates of birth and death of the animal. These methods of bringing closure and relief from grief are not only useful in helping children deal with loss, but they are also utilized by and comforting to adults as well.

Death and Creativity

Death has always engaged the creative energies of talented individuals who are grieving for loved ones. Many artists, poets, musicians, and writers have described in their own media the subtleties of grief. Their creative work brings them peace and offers succor to strangers that are likewise caught up in the web of loss and bereavement. Dogs always inspire us to write and sing about their greatness, loyalty, and courage, not only during their all-too-brief lives, but also in their deaths. Every death of those we love is a little dying of our own as well. No less so is the passing of a beloved animal companion and although the sharp aftermath of death lingers long and hard within us, it, too, *will* pass. With the death of each one of my dogs, I have felt the pang of my own mortality, but I have never felt that they left me completely and forever. The abiding memory of wonderful years with the pack stays and strengthens my resolve to live well and die with courage.

When one of my German shepherds died a few years ago, someone gave me the following poem. I was so moved by the sentiments expressed in the poem that I created a photographic montage as a memorial. The montage included pictures of Geisty as she looked through the years, from birth to death, arranged around the poem. Later, another friend with a multi-dog home lost a dear one from her pack, so I created a memorial montage for her. So it happened that the poem given me during my season of grief has been passed along over and over again, surrounded by beautiful photographs of beloved dogs now deceased. The author is anonymous, but the poem touches everyone who has ever grieved.

> Do not stand at my grave and weep.
> I am not there; I do not sleep.
> I am a thousand winds that blow;
> I am the diamond glint on snow.
> I am the sunlight on ripened grain;
> I am the gentle autumn's rain.
> When you awake in morning's hush,
> I am the swift uplifting rush
> Of quiet birds in circled flight.
> I am the star that shines at night.
> Do not stand at my grave and cry.
> I am not there; I did not die.
>
> —Unknown

Helping Pack Members Deal with the Loss of a Packmate

When you put a dog to sleep, be sure to help its packmates afterwards, for they, too, will suffer the effects of bereavement. In a multi-dog family, deep attachments grow up between the dogs and the death of a pack member touches them all. Dogs can't talk about their feelings or express their grief in words. As pack parents, we have to be aware of their grief and help them deal with the loss.

Be alert for signs of canine depression, listlessness, and lethargy. Beset by grief, dogs sometimes try to hide or spend hours looking out the window as if they are awaiting the return of the pack member that is no more. They may seem timid and afraid to be left alone or cling tenaciously to a pack parent whereas before the death, they were confident and outgoing. Some dogs lose their appetites when a packmate dies. Sadness clouds their eyes and lowers their energy level. The whole demeanor of the pack changes with the death of one member. Surviving pack members might suffer anxiety separation coupled with their grief and sadness. In some situations, as a matter of fact, dogs don't survive their companions very long and they might succumb to death shortly after the passing of a greatly loved pack buddy. Dogs can even die of a broken heart.

It's a big bundle to handle being called upon to comfort other humans in the family, your children, and the remaining dogs in your pack. That's the cost of loving other creatures. I wouldn't have missed it for the world, all the joy and happiness of living with my pack as well as the deep spiritual experience of living with their loss. Never succumb to the denial cycle that sometimes follows loss. Not facing it won't make anything go away.

To alleviate pet pain in the loss of pack partners and to alleviate your own, start by trying to understand that everything you feel is real, and it is not your imagination suggesting that animals also grieve. They do. Let your gentle, kind words of comfort be your first line of defense against the onslaught of grief and bereavement, words directed at your grieving pack but mirrored back to you. Speak to them as to yourself. Say what you feel. Tell them everything is going to be all right. The very sound of your soothing voice is healing in itself. As you hear yourself speaking comforting words to your grieving human family and to the dogs that remain, you'll be surprised at how much those words and tones revert back to you helping to heal your grief as well.

Dr. Wayne Hunthausen, DVM, an animal behavior consultant and recent past president of the American Veterinary Society of Animal Behavior, suggests that distracting surviving pets from their grief behavior by engaging them in play is more appropriate than rushing to hug or cuddle the survivor dog that might be going around the house crying or manifesting other signs of depression and sadness. Dr. Hunthausen said that by trying to make grief-stricken dogs feel better by hugging and coddling them when they display negative grief in the form of pacing, whining, barking, or destructive behavior only exacerbates the problem. The animal can misunderstand your affectionate gestures as a reward for its grief behavior, which might encourage continued whining, pacing, barking and crying. My personal experience, however, was different. My affection and tenderness with the dogs in my pack after one of their members died, seemed to help them not hinder them in overcoming their own sadness. Decide for yourself what works best for your animals. Patience and compassion are absolutely necessary.

Letting your animals see and sniff the deceased before you dispose of its remains can help them through their loss by giving them a chance to say goodbye. Dogs, like wolves and other animals of the wild, have their own instinct for recognizing the finality of death and dealing with it. My dog Grip went through deaths of loved pack members in our household. He was an unbelievably sensitive and intelligent dog, so much so that I often joked with friends that Grip might really be a human boy dressed up in a dog suit. At the death of my oldest female shepherd, Cara Mia, Grip grieved and pined, but Geisty, his daughter, just took over Cara Mia's place on the living room futon. Some years later Geisty died as the result of cardiogenic shock following an automobile accident. Once more, Grip grieved profoundly while my youngest German shepherd, Abby, just took over Geisty's spot on the futon.

Grip's otherwise happy face (he was a dog that genuinely smiled) took on a look of seriousness and sorrow that mirrored my own. My friends and family commented on the depth of Grip's bereavement. I spent many hours sitting beside him and talking to him and I always felt that somehow, Grip understood. Eventually he revived, but I believe he always missed Cara Mia and Geisty, despite Abby's constant attempts to buddy up to him and his obvious pleasure playing with the younger pup.

Our sixteen-year-old Siamese cat, Maximus, died shortly before Geisty's accident. I laid out the body of the cat on a small table where my other animals, Grip, Geisty, and Nikki, a Tonkinese cat, could see and sniff her. Thus, they participated in the finality of Maxi's departure from this life. She was the tiniest adult cat I ever saw, yet the greatest powerhouse of presence imaginable. Max helped me raise every single one of my German shepherd puppies. She was, believe it or not, the mother of my pack. For the dogs, little Max was a constant in their lives, disciplinarian and feline mom nurturing and supervising puppies twice her size!

A week before my dad died, Grip had to be put to sleep following acute kidney failure. He was twelve years old. This time, Abby grieved inconsolably. One week later came the fateful day of September 11, 2001. In the wake of all that sorrow, I found great comfort in my remaining pack, Abby, my German shepherd, Primo, a British Shorthair, and Nikki, my eighteen-year-old Tonkinese. They definitely reflected the grief that surrounded and permeated our lives at this time. The loss of my father and diminishment of my pack, the horror of September 11, the uproar and chaos in the world around us, and the terrible uncertainty of what might lie ahead, created an enormous chasm within us. Many animals helped their people through the aftermath of terrorism that shook our lives at the root.

As other multi-dog people also reported, being at home with the pack was a sanctuary of comfort and healing after the events of September 11. For me, Abby's presence in my life took on a whole new meaning. I worked for weeks to help her through her loss, and all the while, she was doing the same for me. Several months later the death of Nikki diminished our pack further. Nikki was an elder in the pack. She died at home the summer after September 11 at the ripe old age of eighteen years. Although I cremated all the others and retained their ashes, I decided to bury Nikki in a field where we hike. I wrapped her up in an old T-shirt and laid her in a grave I dug myself, well-hidden from view and far away from traffic.

During Nikki's burial, Abby stood by my side. She seemed to understand what was going on as I said a few prayers thanking God for all the enjoyment Nikki's eighteen years had given us. Abby looked up into my face while I completed preparations at the grave and lovingly placed Nikki in the waiting breast of Mother Earth. To this day, many months later, Abby runs directly to the spot where Nikki is buried no matter where I park my car adjacent to that field. She waits for me beneath the tree until I, too, reach Nikki's grave. Then we stand together for a moment and for all the world, I swear Abby seems to know exactly what's going on. Does she?

It's a well-known fact that dogs can detect scent as deep as forty to forty-five feet underground and eighty feet under snow. That's why canines are so good at search and rescue and avalanche work. Abby knows where Nikki lies because she can still find Nikki's scent there, and since my cats were pack-mates with my dogs, there remains a deep bond connecting all of us together.

Dogs need time to heal after grief, but they *do* heal, and life goes on. It will be different, however, without the ones that have gone before, but there will be others. There surely must. That's the rhythm of the universe. These irrevocable finalities are hard to understand and like all the mysteries of life they must be embraced with resignation and acceptance. Of course, if I could bring them back for just one moment one more time, truly I would, and so would you with your pack children now departed. Nevertheless, in the final analysis, even if we *could* restore life to the precious beings we have lost, would we not have to part with them all over again? "Everything that lives must die." Animals don't know the words but they live the reality of their instinctual ability to handle death and dying. We must do the same.

What is a dog, if not an absolute friend? In 1870, Senator George Vest wrote this piece, "Tribute to a Dog." For me these words spell out the nature of this deepest human attachment to another species. As one's pack is slowly diminished when dog after dog passes away, George Vest's words help us celebrate the memories left behind of pack life as we knew it.

Tribute to a Dog

The one absolutely unselfish friend that man can have in this selfish world, the one that never deserts him, the one that never proves ungrateful or treacherous, is his dog. A man's dog stands by him in prosperity and in poverty, in health and in sickness. He will sleep on the cold ground, where the wintry winds blow and the snow drives fiercely, if only he may be near his master's side. He will kiss the hand that has no food to offer; he will lick the wounds and sores that come in encounter with the roughness of the world. He guards the sleep of his pauper master as if he were a prince. When all other friends desert, he remains. When riches take wings and reputation falls to pieces, he is as constant in his love as the sun in its journey through the heavens.

—Senator George Vest, 1870

Epilogue

To have lived among dogs is one of the greatest enhancements of our human journey. For all the eons that people have shared their lives with domesticated canines, making together a common hearth and home, humans have been enriched by this interspecies bond forged in loyalty and love, unbreakable in this world except by the perversity of people. Dogs are always true and constant, faithful to the end, needing only the opportunity to be so. Perhaps, the link we share with our dogs is unbreakable in the next world as well.

Although they are *not* children, but another species, noble and unique unto themselves, not inferior, not brute beasts, but creatures of another kind, dogs do seem at times to become for us "other children," and we, for them, pack parents. There's nothing wrong with thinking of yourself as a parent figure for your dogs. We are their alphas and they are our pack. That's the whole of it, this human-canine family that has made its way across the horizon of time merging one life with another, their species with ours. Like sky and earth, air and water, dogs and people are joined together in the oneness and unity of the universe. Traveling forward, our pack and ourselves, we move through the years like a team walking side by side together through all the precarious places of life's great journey. We share a common destiny with our dogs, intimacy and pain, ecstasy and sorrow. We work together and play together, live together and die together. Joy and heartache echo in this interspecies bond that transcends anything we can ever say about it. It's only the heart that grasps the whole story.

Dogs will certainly remain the cherished companions of the human race for as long as human and canine life endures on this planet, and perhaps beyond. There will surely be more and greater advances in the evolution of both of our species, and perhaps, in the fullness of time, we, the People of the Pack, will have evolved to the same level of incorruptibility, loyalty, faithful love, and devotion that even now, our dogs give to us. If only we could be all they think we are! *That* is the enrichment and challenge that is ours. Owning a pack of dogs is an opportunity to observe the simplicity of creatures that feel at home in the universe, satisfied and content with their lot.

Only human beings fail in incorruptibility, loyalty, faithful love, and devotion, for we, alone, are plagued by the miseries of ego and attachment. We alone suffer the fragmentation of deception. Isn't it remarkable that so many people consider dogs lesser creatures than themselves, yet canines living among us may well be here for the sole purpose of teaching us the lessons of the pack: acceptance of one's place in the scheme of things and recognition that there are always larger and greater than ourselves. From the pack we should learn respect for alpha and the rule of law, fairness and strength in power, incorruptibility in the face of temptation and loyalty that endures to the very end. Dogs might well be here, after all, just to show us the simple truth of faithful love, uncomplicated by ego or attachment. As People of the Pack, we are fortunate in having such great teachers, these four-legged furry examples of fidelity and true devotion. Dogs are not 'lesser beings' than ourselves, but only different ones, creatures capable of bonding with us beyond our power to comprehend, here with us to show the way, protectors in the night, fellow travelers in our long journey toward the Light.

Resources for Multi-Dog Households

n the process of learning how to care properly for the pack, you'll benefit enormously from checking out the many helpful resources available. Perhaps you've already tapped into many of them. A wise pet parent will strive to learn as much as possible every step of the way. You can't use the plethora of available resources all at once. Gradually, though, you'll find yourself welcoming new opportunities to increase your canine knowledge, and in the process—yup, you guessed it—you'll probably end up in pursuit of another dog to add to your multi-dog home.

Books

Aloff, Brenda. *Aggression in Dogs: Practical Management, Prevention & Behavior Modification*. Wenatchee, Washington: Dogwise Publishing, 2002.

Barwig, Susan, Asa Mays, D.V.M., and Brenda E. Abbott. *The German Shepherd Book*. Wheat Ridge, Colorado: Hoflin Publishing, 1986.

Barwig, Susan and Stewart Hilliard. *Schutzhund Theory and Training Methods*. New York: Howell Book House, 1991.

Baer, Nancy and Steve Duno. *Leader of the Pack: How to Take Control of Your Relationship with Your Dog.* New York: Harper Collins, 1996.

Bielakiewicz, Gerilyn J. *The Everything® Dog Training and Tricks Book: Turn the Most Mischievous Canine into a Well-Behaved Dog Who Knows a Few Tricks.* Avon, Massachusetts: Adams Media, 2002.

Billinghurst, Ian. *Give Your Dog a Bone.* Ian Billinghurst, 1993.

Bonham, Margaret H. *Introduction to Dog Agility.* New York: Barrows Educational Services, 2000.

Bonham, Margaret H. *Simple Guide to Getting Active with Your Dog.* Neptune City, New Jersey: T.F.H., 2003.

Booth, Sheila. *Purely Positive Training.* Ridgefield, Connecticut: Podium Publications, 1998.

Booth, Sheila and Gottfried Dildei. *Training in Drive: Schutzhund Obedience.* Ridgefield, Connecticut: Podium Publications, 1992.

Brunke, Dawn Baumann. *Animal Voices: Telepathic Communication in the Web of Life.* Rochester, Vermont: Bear & Company, 2002.

Bryson, Sandy. *Search Dog Training.* Pacific Grove, California: Boxwood Press, 1988.

Bulanda, Susan. *Ready to Serve, Ready to Save: Strategies of Real-Life Search and Rescue Missions.* Phoenix, Arizona: Doral Publishing, Inc., 1999.

Carlson, Delbert G. and James M. Giffin. *Dog Owner's Home Veterinary Handbook.* New York: Howell House, 1980.

Climer, Jerry. *How to Raise a Dog When Nobody's Home.* 2nd Edition. Penny Dreadful Press, 1995.

Clothier, Suzanne. *Bones Would Rain from the Sky: Deepening Our Relationships with Dogs.* New York: Warner Books, 2003.

Coile, D. Carolina, Ph.D., *Beyond Fetch: Fun, Interactive Activities for You and Your Dog.* New York: Howell Book House, 2003.

Coren, Stanley. *How to Speak Dog: Mastering the Art of Dog-Human Communication.* Fireside, 2001.

Davis, Christine. *For Every Dog an Angel: The Forever Dog.* Portland, Oregon: Lighthearted Press, 1997.

Donaldson, Jean. *The Culture Clash.* Oakland, California: James and Kenneth Publishers, Inc., 1997.

Edelstein, Barney. *Obedience and Tracking Today.* Wheat Ridge, Colorado: Hoflin Publishing, 1989.

Evans, Job Michael. *Evans Guide for Counseling Dog Owners.* New York: Howell Book House, 1986.

Evans, Job Michael. *Civilized City Canines.* New York: Howell Book House, 1988.

Evans, Job Michael. *People, Pooches, and Problems: Understanding, Controlling and Correcting Problem Behavior in Your Dog.* New York: Howell Book House, 2001.

Fennel, Jan. *The Dog Listener: How to Communicate with Your Dog for Willing Cooperation.* New York, New York: HarperResource, 2001.

Fields-Babineau, Miriam. *Multiple Dog Households*. Neptune City, New Jersey: T.F.H. Publications, Inc., 2001.

Fisher, Betty and Suzanne Delzio. *So Your Dog's Not Lassie: Tips for Training the Independent and Difficult Breeds*. New York: Harper Collins, 1998.

Flaim, Denise. *Holistic Dog Book: Canine Care for the Twenty-First Century*. New York: Howell Book House, 2003.

Fogle, Bruce and Anne B. Wilson. *The Dog's Mind: Understanding Your Dog's Behavior*. New York: Howell Book House, 1992.

Fogle, Bruce and Amanda Williams. *First Aid for Dogs: What to Do When Emergencies Happen*. New York: Penguin U.S.A., 1997.

Gardiner, Andrew. *First Aid for Dogs*. London, England: J.A. Allen & Co., Ltd., 2002.

Grayson, Fred N. and Chris Kingsley. *The Portable Petswelcome.com: A Complete Guide to Traveling with Your Pet*. New York: Howell Book House, 2001.

Habgood, Dawn and Robert Habgood. *On the Road Again with Man's Best Friend*. 2nd Edition. Duxbury, Massachusetts: Dawbert Press, 2003.

Habgood, Dawn and Robert Habgood. *Pets on the Go: The Definitive Pet Accommodation and Vacation Guide*. Duxbury, Massachusetts: Dawbert Press, 2002.

Hart, Ernest H. *The German Shepherd Dog*. Neptune City, New Jersey: T.F.H. Publications, Inc., 1985.

Katz, John. *A Dog Year: Twelve Months, Four Dogs, and Me.* New York: Random House, 2003.

Knapp, Caroline. *Pack of Two: The Intricate Bond Between People and Dogs.* New York: Dell Publishing, Random House, 1995.

Koehler, William. *Guard Dog Training.* New York: Howell Book Company, 1987.

Koehler, William R. *The Koehler Method of Training Tracking Dogs.* New York: Hungry Minds, Inc., 1984.

Kowalski, Gary. *Goodbye, Friend: Healing Wisdom for Anyone Who Has Ever Lost a Pet.* Walpole, New Hampshire: Stillpoint Publishing, 1997.

Lanting, Fred. *The Total German Shepherd Dog.* Loveland, Colorado: Alpine Publications, Inc., 1990.

Levy, Juliette De Bairacli. *The Complete Herbal Handbook for the Dog and Cats.* 6th Edition. London, England: Faber & Faber, 1995.

Link and Crowley. *Following the Pack: The World of Wolf Research.* Stillwater, Minnesota: Voyageur Press, 1994.

Lonsdale, Tom. *Raw Meaty Bones Promote Health.* Sydney, Australia: Rivetco P/L, 1991.

Lopez, Barry H. *Of Wolves and Men.* New York: Charles Scribner's Sons, 1978.

Masson, Jeffrey Moussaieff. *Dogs Never Lie About Love.* New York: Crown Publishers, Inc., 1997.

McConnell, Patricia, Ph.D. *Cautious Canine.* Fort Lauderdale, Florida: Dogs' Best Friend, Inc., 1998.

McConnell, Patricia, Ph.D. *The Other End of the Leash.* New York: Ballantine Books, 2003.

Mech, David L. *Artic Wolf: Ten Years with the Pack.* Stillwater, Minnesota: Voyager Press, 1997.

Messonnier, Shawn, D.V.M. *Natural Health Bible for Dogs & Cats.* New York: Prima Publishing, 2001.

Miller, Pat. *Power of Positive Dog Training.* New York: Howell Book House, 2001.

Morgan, Diane. *Feeding Your Dog for Life: The Real Facts About Proper Nutrition.* Phoenix, Arizona: Doral Publishing Co., 2002.

Myers, Arthur. *Communicating with Animals: The Spiritual Connection with Animals.* New York: McGraw-Hill/ Contemporary Press, 1997.

Nicholas, Anna Katherine. *The Book of the German Shepherd Dog.* Neptune City, New Jersey: T.F.H. Publications, Inc., 1983.

O'Driscoll, Catherine. *What Vets Don't Tell You About Vaccines.* Alberta, Canada: Our Pets' Inc., 1993.

O'Neil, Jacqueline. *All About Agility.* Revised Edition. New York: Howell Book House, Inc., 1999.

Owens, Paul, and Norma Eckroate. *The Dog Whisperer: A Compassionate, Nonviolent Approach to Dog Training.* Avon, Massachusetts: Adams Media, 1999.

Padgett, George A. *Control of Canine Genetic Diseases.* New York: Howell Book House, Inc., 1998.

Patterson, Gary. *Tracking: From the Beginning.* Englewood, Colorado: Sirius Publishing, 1992.

Paulsen, Gary. *Winterdance: The Fine Madness of Running the Iditarod.* New York: A Harvest Book, Harcourt Brace & Company, 1994.

Pearsall, Milo D. and Hugo Verbruggen, M.D. *Scent: Training to Track, Search, and Rescue.* Loveland, Colorado: Alpine Publications, Inc., 1982.

Pitcairn, Richard H. and Susan Bubble Pitcairn. *Dr. Pitcairn's Complete Guide to Natural Health For Dogs & Cats.* Emmaus, Pennsylvania: Rodale Press, 1995.

Pope, Raphaela. *Wisdom of the Animals.* Avon, Massachusetts: Adams Media, 2001.

Pryor, Karen. *Don't Shoot the Dog.* New York: Bantam Doubleday Dell Pub., 1999.

Rose, Tom and Gary Patterson. *Teaching the Competitive Working Dog.* Englewood, Colorado: Giblaut Publishing Company, 1985.

Rugaas, Turid. *On Talking Terms with Dogs: Calming Signals.* [This book is important because it helps the pack owner understand how to interpret dog body signals within the social hierarchy and assists in resolving conflict within the pack.] Carlsborg, Washington: Legacy-By-Mail, Inc., 1997.

Schellenberg, Dietmar. *Top Working Dogs: A Training Manual.* Webster, New York: D.B.C., 1982.

Schoen, Allen M., D.V.M. *Love, Miracles, and Animal Healing.* New York: Simon and Schuster, 1995.

Schoen, Allen M., D.V.M. and Susan G. Wynn. *Complementary and Alternative Veterinary Medicine: Principles and Practice*. Philadelphia, Pennsylvania: Mosby, 1998.

Schul, Bill. *The Psychic Power of Animals*. New York: Fawcett Publications, 1977.

Schultze, Kymythy. *Natural Nutrition for Dogs and Cats: The Ultimate Diet*. Carlsbad, California: Hay House, Inc., 1999.

Schwartz, Cheryl, D.V.M. *Natural Healing for Dogs and Cats A–Z*. Carlsbad, California: Hay House, Inc., 2000.

Shearer, Tamara S., D.V.M. and Stanford Apseloff. *Emergency First Aid for Dogs*. 3rd Edition. Columbus, Ohio: Ohio Distinctive Publishers, Inc., 1996.

Simmons-Moake, Jane. *Agility Training: The Fun Sport for All Dogs*. New York: Howell Book House, Inc., 1992.

Smith, Penelope. *Animals: Our Return to Wholeness*. Point Reyes, California: Pegasus Publications, 1993.

Steiger, Brad, and Sherry Hansen Steiger. *Dog Miracles: Inspirational and Heroic True Stories*. Avon, Massachusetts, 2001.

Stein, Diane. *Natural Healing for Dogs and Cats*. Freedom, California: Crossing Press, 1993.

Theberge, John. *Wolf Country: Eleven Years Tracking the Algonquin Packs*. Toronto, Ontario, Canada: McClelland & Stewart, 1998.

Traveling with Your Pet: The AAA Pet Book. Heathrow, Florida: AAA Publishing, 1999.

Tucker, Toni and Judith Adler. *Zen Dog*. New York: Clarkson Potter, 2001.

Volhard, Wendy and Kerry Brown. *Holistic Guide for a Healthy Dog*. 2nd Edition. New York: Howell Book House, Inc., 2000.

Walkowicz, Chris. *The German Shepherd Dog*. Fairfax, Virginia: Denlinger's Publishers, Inc., 1990.

Walters, Heather MacLean. *Take Your Pet Along: 1001 Places to Stay with Your Pet*. M.C.E., 2001.

Weaver, Helen. *The Daisy Sutra: Conversations with My Dog*. Woodstock, New York: Buddha Rock Press, 2003.

Wolff, Hans Gunter. *Homeopathic Medicine for Dogs: A Handbook for Vets and Pet Owners*. London, England: The C.W. Daniel Co., Inc., 1998.

Wulff-Tilford, Mary L. and Gregory Tilford. *Herbs for Pets: All You Ever Wanted to Know*. Irvine, California: Bowtie Press, 1999.

Videos

Battaglia, Carmelo. *Choosing the Best Puppy*.

Bloeme, Peter. *Frisbee Dogs*. Inner Visions Group, 1993.

Dunbar, Ian. *Dog Training for Children*.

Frost, April. *Training That Works for Your Dog*. Increase Video Studio, 1995.

Margolis, Matthew. *Woof: It's a Dog's Life*. WGBH Boston Video, 1999.

Myrow, Jeff and Ed Spiegel. *Video Guide to Dogs: How to Select the Perfect Canine Companion.* Fast Forward Marketing, 1996.

Teach Me Please – Easy as 1-2-3 Dog Training.

Tellington-Jones, Linda. *Unleash Your Dog's Potential.* 2001.

Those Wonderful Dogs, National Geographic. 1997.

White, Linda. *Puppy Smart's Lessons for a Lifetime.* 2003.

Web Sites

www.animalvoices.net

www.canineauto.com

www.canismajor.com

www.dogcross.com

www.dogfriendly.com

www.doghouse.com

www.doginfomat.com

www.dogpatch.org

www.dog-play.com

www.dogwise.com

www.flyingdogpress.com

www.griefhealing.com

www.hemopet.com

www.inthecompanyofdogs.com

www.k9web.com

www.pawsacrossamerica.com

www.petswelcome.com

www.petvacations.com

www.rovinwithrover.com

www.shirleys-welness-cafe.com

www.takeyourpet.com

www.traveldog.com

www.woofs.org

Additional Resources

The following items can be purchased directly from the author by e-mailing your request to *geisty@verizon.net.*

Doggie identification cards: Wallet-sized laminated doggie identification cards, as described in Chapter 10.

Pet memorials: Ready-to-frame pet memorial with several favorite photos of your dog(s). Your choice of poem: "Do Not Stand at My Grave and Weep" or "The Rainbow Bridge". Scanning, design, and printing included in price. Sizes: 8" x 10" ($15.00), 11" x 14" ($25.00).

T-shirts: Original designs. Custom-made for you and your pack. Top quality white T-shirts, Adults: S, M, L, XL, and 2X. Children's sizes also available.

Index

About the Author

Theresa Mancuso is a writer, photographer, and graphic designer whose love for animals has followed her throughout the long journeys of childhood and adolescence (which seems to have never ended in her case), into the convent and monastery and out again after twenty-two years of religious community life, and currently in the halls of New York City government. She has enormous capacity for sharing home and heart (and office when she can get away with it) with her beloved four-legged furry critters, canine and feline, with whom she has created a family, inspiration for several books, dozens of articles, and thousands of photographs and T-shirts.

Theresa creates animal theme T-shirts for kids in her neighborhood, which she distributes at will, sometimes surprising them with photos of themselves. The cover of *Who Moved My Bone?* is available on a T-shirt, thanks to her generous publisher. Theresa hopes to be buried in a black T-shirt on which in tiny white letters reads: "Holy Shit! I'm dead." Or: "Good bye, I had a wonderful time!"

For more than thirty years, Theresa has been a spiritual counselor for dozens of individuals of every faith and no faith. She has worked with every race, gender, sexual orientation, and belief or nonbelief. She regularly supports and assists hundreds of people in their diverse spiritual journeys. It all goes to the same place, she says.

If you wish to contact Theresa Mancuso for any purpose arising from her diverse interests and skills, or simply to tell her what you think of this book, please feel free to write to her at the following e-mail address: *geisty@verizon.net.*